Start, Grow, and Expand Your Holistic Health Business

Dawn Fleming

Energy Transformations, llc.
1202 N. Oxbow Dr.
Dewey, AZ 86327
U.S.A.

reikidawn@yahoo.com

http://www.energytransformations.org

ISBN: 978-0-578-19310-6

Author
Dawn Fleming

Editors
William W. Fleming, Jr. and Fran Walsh

Technical Assistance/Cover Design
Amanda Sachs

INTRODUCTION

Many professional holistic health providers have trained long and hard, putting in many hours of study and practice to learn valuable skills and techniques to help others. Some chose this as a first career before getting experience in the business arena. Upon graduation, the holistic practitioner is often left on his/her own to start a viable and thriving business without any road map or previous experience in business and marketing. He/She may take wrong turns along the path to establishing and growing a thriving business and become discouraged. The practitioner may decide to work at a wellness center or spa in order to learn the business end of creating success in their future holistic health business. Whether you choose to work independently or in a spa or wellness center, you want to start off with a good understanding of your options and how to begin to grow and expand your business.

Other holistic health professionals choose this career field later in life as a second or even third career. They benefit from their previous life experiences, but can also find that holistic health is a unique field and does not always follow other business models. Working in the field of holistic health requires professionals to tap into their inner resources of creativity and intuition as well as to continue the outer work that needs to be accomplished in order to create success.

Most of us did not declare that we were going to grow up to be holistic healing professionals when we were planning our future careers. When I was in school, most of these careers did not exist. Some of us found these careers in mid-life. Somehow we were introduced to this area and it became our new direction. It found us. It might have begun as a new interest or hobby. We began reading everything that we could get our hands on that would explain what we were experiencing. Our reading was the beginning of a new career path.

Friends introduced me to Chakra Balancing in 1989. My daughter had been diagnosed with a health condition that was not responding to the doctor's course of action. We decided to try Chakra Balancing and we immediately began seeing results. One day I was invited to watch. I began sensing and feeling the energy that was occurring. From then on, I was hooked and I began attending every meeting to receive training. I soon found myself working on anyone who gave me permission. I became a Reiki Master and developed into a Medical Intuitive. In December 2001, I walked away from my government career to take my part time business and grow it into a full time energy business.

Reiki, Medical Intuition, Sound Therapy, Life Coaching and mentoring are a few of the services I offer. I want to share it with those who will benefit from receiving what I've learned. It is who I am. It is sometimes challenging, always interesting, fun, and it provides plenty of room for self-discovery and growth. Within two years of leaving my government job, my clients tripled. All of the classes that I taught were filled as well. I used my business background and experience over the years to build and expand my business.

This book is focused on you, the holistic entrepreneur. No matter what stage your business is in, there is valuable information to help you move to the next level. This book will guide you through the inner and outer work that it takes to create, grow, and expand your business. By fully participating in the exercises, you will create a clear vision of what you want to offer, thereby aligning yourself energetically with your vision. In addition, the exercises will offer many opportunities and strategies for increasing your clientele. I believe that we should enjoy what we are doing in life. This book will help you get there so that you can do what you love.

In this book I refer to starters, growers, and expanders. Starters are those practitioners or therapists who are at the very beginning of birthing their business. Growers already have a few clients; however, they have a lot more to do to get their business where they want it. Expanders have an established business and are ready to strengthen themselves and venture into new territories. At the end of many of the chapters, there is advice for those who are starters, growers and expanders.

As holistic practitioners, we know that our success is another person's healing. Healing on any level provides healing for the world. We are world light workers and we are here not only to serve, but also to be abundant. If I can create a fulfilling and abundant business, anyone with determination, creativity, and perseverance can, too.

May you be a light for many,

Dawn Fleming

ACKNOWLEDGEMENTS

I want to thank all of my clients, near and far, who have brought me so much joy doing what I love and have helped me to build an amazing business.

I want to thank my incredible husband Bill Fleming who is always right there to support my ideas, offer good advice, and provide lots of unconditional love.

Many thanks to my daughters Amanda and Vicki who have been on this journey with me and are incredible Reiki Masters in their own right.

Thank you to the Divine force and source from which this book and workshops flowed. God is the greatest of all Directors and Writers. It was a labor of love.

Contents

GETTING STARTED

Many people have said to me, "I really want to have a business like yours," but when I hear them talk about what they want to do or how they are going about making it a reality, I find that their plan of action seems unfocused. They are sending out a message to the universe that they are not sure what it is that they want. Some make it sound as if their massage or energy practice is something they dabble in and others make it out to be their personal obsession or hobby. Others state they want a full-time business, but are not willing to commit to the work to make it happen. Believe me—it doesn't just happen.

Starting your own holistic health business takes work, creativity, and continuous learning of what does and does not work. It takes time, refinement and an ability to flow with change. It also requires inner strength and outer follow-through. When you make this commitment, the way you handle your business will change. However, there are some valuable first steps that will make a tremendous difference in creating a successful holistic health business.

When you truly get into the mindset of expanding or growing your business, almost every place you go provides opportunities or information for you to expand your business. Say, for instance, that you are in the dentist's office. The person next to you begins to talk, you introduce yourself and as you tell her what you do, you offer her your business card. Then you let the dental hygienist know what you do, as well as the dentist. You leave them some business cards. If there is real interest, you follow up with a call, an email, or you drop off some flyers and brochures. While sitting in the office you see a local health newspaper. You pick it up and read the ads to see the different ways people promote their services. You see a health fair advertised and make note of the number to call to set up a table or rent space for your table. You also see a calendar of events for a local hospital and it lists support groups for certain health conditions. So you copy down a few numbers because you want to contact someone about doing a talk to educate the members of that support group about the benefit of your holistic health modality.

In my last book *Creating a Successful Holistic Health Practice*, I learned that a lot of energy workers and massage therapists were not seeing their practice as a business. It is a business. Isn't this what supports you? The wording *practice* for many does not mean business, but when you depend on this for your income, it is a business. A lot of spiritual people do not like the word *business* and avoid it. However, those who are successful at what they do in this realm, have no issue with using the word *business* to describe their services. When we treat what we are doing as a business, success is guaranteed.

A professional holistic healing career needs to be seen and approached emotionally, mentally and physically in the same way that any professional career field is approached. No one is going to find you and make you an overnight sensation. Instead, think of yourself as an entrepreneur who needs to find your inner motivator and get moving in the right direction. You will at times solicit good financial and legal advice. However, you have to be your own boss, motivator, secretary, and fan club.

So where do we start? There is no one perfect place to start. That's because our life circumstances will give us different starting points. So work with the information presented here and use it in a way that works with where you are in your process. The information included in *Start, Grow, and Expand Your Holistic Health Business* is intended to help any holistic entrepreneur, from those who work in a spa, salon or holistic center, to those who work out of their homes or private offices. The ideas, exercises, and information presented here will work in a variety of settings.

Am I Ready for a Holistic Health Career?

So you've earned your massage license, Healing Touch or Reiki certificate, yoga certification or acupuncture degree and you're now ready to grow a business. Here are some preliminary questions to ask yourself:

- How much experience do you have?
- Do you know the state and federal laws regulating your career field?
- Can you articulate what you do so that others can understand it?
- Do you fear not having money?
- Are you self-motivated?
- Do you have healthy self-esteem?
- Can you think outside the box?

How much experience do you have? In order to go out on your own and build your business, experience is important. One of the first questions that clients will ask is, "How long you have been doing this?" They might also ask if there is an area in which you are specialized. If you do not have experience, you need to get it. Start by putting in the hours: you can volunteer your services at senior centers, hospitals, or in the school clinic where you received training. You can also work on friends and family. The more people you work on, the better you are able to understand the dynamics of your field. Getting hands-on practice will enhance your ability to talk about what you are experiencing with your clients in a way they can understand. When you can speak from experience, clients will perceive you as knowledgeable and provide you with referrals. Occasionally in my classes, I have people who take Reiki I and want to go out and open a business the next day. I tell them that when they leave my class, they can do Reiki on themselves and others. Be aware that when you start charging money for your services, your clients will expect you to be experienced and will have a perceived notion about what kind of results they should receive from your service.

Do you know the state and federal laws regulating your career field? Most states have laws regulating chiropractics, acupuncture, massage, nursing, social work, counselors, and naturopathic doctors. A few states have laws regulating the modalities that fall under the term energy work, such as Reiki, Healing Touch, Rolfing, Shiatsu, etc. Don't assume that being ignorant of the laws is a way around state and federal regulations. You can find most of the requirements for these fields on the web at the State or National Board representing your field. When it comes to the realms of energy work, you should contact your local government to find out where the laws stand.

Some states require energy workers to have a national certification or licensing in nursing, social work, acupuncture, massage or chiropractics in order to receive money for doing Reiki, Healing Touch, etc. Some energy workers get ordained in a non-denominational church or religious order so that they can perform hands-on healing. Make sure you find out whether this is a legitimate avenue and whether it would hold up in the court system.

Can you articulate what you do so that others can understand it and be interested enough to try it? If you want to generate clients, you need to be comfortable talking about your career, your gifts, and your experiences. Anyone could be a potential client. So you need to express what it is that you do and how that person might benefit from it. Often you only have a minute or two to do this. Find phrases that will pique a potential client's interest to request a session, classes or more information. Find ways to be adept at talking to different audiences, i.e. medical personnel versus the layperson. Make sure you use laypersons' language (terminology and ideas) so your audience can easily understand and so they'll be interested in your skills or teaching. As you read further, you'll find additional suggestions for ways to articulate your ideas as well as ways to connect with prospective clients.

Do you fear not having money? If this is a fear, it's a good idea to look it straight in the eye and work with letting it go. Ask yourself why you are pursuing a holistic health career. Most of us would say that we have been led to this path. If this is the case for you, then simply remind yourself that Spirit would not bring you here to fail. Dwelling on fear can end up blocking the energy of success by inviting negativity into your journey. Fear-based thinking has a way of slowing your momentum and is more likely to result in failure than in success. The abundance will flow when you align your mind and emotions with the knowledge that you are serving a Higher Plan and when you follow through with the appropriate actions. When you are in alignment with your true nature, without fear, pathways to abundance will open.

Are you self-motivated and self-disciplined? If you are not self-motivated and self-disciplined, find another career path. Being a successful practitioner, whether you work for yourself or for a salon or holistic center, will depend on the degree to which you can motivate yourself to make contacts and do the follow-up work that will lead to clients/students.

What about your self-esteem? If your self-esteem is low, you are limiting your success. You need to think enough of yourself to know the value of what you have to offer and to charge accordingly. Healthy self-esteem also allows the practitioner to have healthy boundaries. If you have major self-esteem issues, give some serious thought to addressing them before you take on clients. No one is going to feel good about getting services from someone who displays low self-esteem.

Can you think outside the box? Working in the holistic healing field means that you function outside the parameters of the 9:00-5:00 workday. In order to create success, you'll need to think outside the traditional business models. As a matter of fact, let's get rid of the box altogether! Tap into your intuitive nature. Network not only to gain clients and students but also to learn from others about the pros and cons of working in the holistic health field. Make adjustments based on your personal preferences and those of your clients and students. Always be ready to learn from mistakes and to try something new.

If you know that this is your life's work, then I truly encourage you to go forward and to be successful in helping others to heal. No other calling or career provides such satisfaction and growth for both the client and practitioner. If you're still not sure whether you're cut out to be a holistic health provider, check out the 10 indicators below. Being an entrepreneur in the holistic health arena might *not* be a good fit for you if:

- You fear not having money
- You have issues about accepting money for holistic health services
- You constantly make excuses about why you cannot reach your goals
- You wait for others to do the things that you need to do for yourself
- You have low self-esteem
- You have poor boundaries
- You depend on others to validate your ideas
- You do not love what you do
- People get on your nerves easily
- You have poor communication skills

Be honest with yourself. Can you address these issues by getting some coaching or counseling? Are you willing to make the changes needed in order to be successful?

In order to begin or to refine the journey of being a successful holistic care provider, let's start with defining your vision for your business. If you do not yet have a clear vision, then you could be sending mixed signals to your clients, your family, and the universe. When you get clear on what you want to create, your vision will steer you in the right direction to making it all a reality.

Vision Declaration

A great place to start in creating success is creating a vision of what you want. Clarity in knowing what you want to create is key. When you gain clarity, you align your intentions with your vision and eliminate the scattered energies that occur when you try to maintain a vision that is too broad or too narrow. So ask yourself, "In what I am pursuing, what does success look like and feel like?" Begin by taking a few moments to close your eyes and put together a picture of how success would look and feel. After a few moments, write down your thoughts in a journal or notebook.

Now that you have some new information to work with, the next step is to condense it into about four to eight sentences that you can easily hold in your mind and share with others. Go through the above information and pull out the key ideas. Write those down now.

Your next step is to turn the above information into your Vision Declaration. I refer to it as a "declaration" instead of a statement because statement sounds flat and one-dimensional. "Declaration" sounds as if you are sending this vision out to the world and out to the Universe for support. You are declaring that this is what will be! Look at the words you have used above to describe your vision. Are they strong verbs and concise words or are they passive? Choose strong active verbs to describe your vision. Make sure that you word your Vision Declaration as if you are already living that vision. For example, begin with "I am … " or "I perform…"

Take some time now to revise your Vision Declaration using strong verbs and keeping your statements in the present tense.

You will have another opportunity to firm up your vision declaration at the end of the book in the chapter titled Vision Declaration

Revisited. For right now, you can use the Vision Declaration you've crafted. Some practitioners put their final vision statements in a frame and put them on the wall in their workspace with their certificates or in their date books. What works to bring about your Vision Declaration is to hold this vision in your mind each day and focus on it for a minute. Ask your guides to support this vision or something better in alignment with the highest good for you and your clients. If you do Reiki or a form of energy work, send Reiki to the realization of your vision. Each morning and evening read your Vision Declaration out loud and for a moment, hold a vision of the end result. As you do this, feel what it would feel like to fully realize this vision. When you finish, give thanks to all those who support this vision: your family, clients, friends, teachers, spirit guides, angels, ascended masters, etc. You will be amazed at how this exercise will accelerate the realization of your vision. (See Appendix I for examples of Vision Declaration, Goals, and Affirmations.)

Goals

The next step is setting some goals that directly relate to your Vision Declaration. A Harvard study showed that only 3% of the population writes down their goals. This same 3% controls 97% of the world's wealth. Anyone can set goals; so get started.

Take a moment in the quiet of your day or evening and ask yourself, "What are my goals for the next three months?" or "What are the next steps in expanding my business or getting it started?" Close your eyes and ask yourself, "What do I need to accomplish in the next three months in order to realize my vision?" It is important to create a space that allows you to focus on the exercises without distractions so that you can access accurate information that helps you in acquiring success. Write down all the ideas that come to you.

Exercise 1: Creating Your Goals – List any ideas regarding your immediate goals

Your goals are important because they are the guiding steps to bringing your vision into reality. Take the information above and write three to eight short goal statements. With each statement ask yourself, "Is this goal aligned with my vision?" If it is not aligned, you may need to decide whether it is a personal goal or business goal. If it is a business goal, you might need to redo your Vision Declaration. If it is not business, remove it from your goal section.

Keep your Vision Declaration and goals on the same piece of paper. Post them in different places, such as in your scheduling book, near your computer and under your pillow. You want your goals to reflect the steps you are taking to build your business to success. These goals are your "to do" list in generating business. Aligning your Vision Declaration and goals is very important because it provides a road map for achieving success in manifesting the career and business that support what you want to be about. It also helps you to communicate a clear signal so that the energy you are putting into your business is aligned with your vision and goals.

When you finish reading this book, you'll want to revisit the many suggestions contained here for generating success. It's especially important to review this section and to put some more thought into incorporating the ideas here. List your goals in the order that they need to occur. What are three goals you will begin and or complete this week. Write three more for the next week. You should revisit your goals at the end of each week in order to refine your focus and to reflect on what goals you might need to add to or delete from the list.

Affirmations

Read over the goals you generated above in order to create some positive affirmations. The thoughts in your mind create your reality. The more positive energy you put into something, the more quickly it will manifest in your life. Always state your affirmations in the present tense as if they are already happening and always state them in a positive way. If your goal is to have 16 clients a week, your affirmation could be, "I now have 16 paying clients a week." If your goal is to complete your business advertising material, your affirmation might be, "I have completed the advertising for [insert your company name], which is now attracting new and positive business." At the end of your affirmations, repeat the statement, "This or something better for the highest good of all." Make a couple of powerful affirmations that are in alignment with your goals and vision. State these every day as you reflect on your vision and goals.

When you feel you have them the way you want them to read, write them on a separate piece of paper or type them on your computer and post these affirmations in your date book and near your computer. Work with repeating these after you hold your Vision Declaration in your mind. Affirmations send out positive energy to the universe and align you energetically, physically, and mentally with the circumstances and steps you need to take to achieve success.

As you work toward taking the steps to create your vision, leave room for Spirit to do its work in bringing about your success. While it's important to begin taking all the practical and mental steps to ensure success, you also need to remain open to receiving Spirit's help in whatever way it is manifested. Your success may not unfold in exactly the way you think it should. A few times I was disappointed because certain things did not happen in the order or time frame that I had expected, only to be pleasantly surprised later by how things actually unfolded.

Defining the Perfect Client for Your Business

What you might find when you first start your business is that your strong desire for any paying clients can attract the type of clients you might not want. Setting the intention that you just want clients, any clients who are willing to pay, may mean that you need to be prepared for the diverse array you may end up attracting. You might end up with clients who do not show up on time or not at all or those who are looking for you to "fix" them without their participation. You might end up frustrated by last minute cancellations or faced with clients who are unwilling to participate in the healing process.

In order to avoid such situations, spend some time defining "the perfect client" for you and your business. Instead of putting out to the universe a message that says "bring them all on," spend some time exploring who might benefit most from what you have to offer, and also reflect on what type of client would cause you less stress and frustration. So as you begin to draw more clients into your practice, ask yourself, "Who is my perfect client?" Write your thoughts on who your perfect client is.

Here are a few ideas regarding the perfect client. The perfect client shows up on time and keeps all his/her appointments. The perfect client knows that he or she is a participant in the healing process and does everything possible to facilitate healing. The perfect client is open to the learning that is unfolding. The perfect client respects client/practitioner boundaries.

The perfect client is willing to live consciously and is open to communicate. The perfect client continues to receive my services while they are needed and provides referrals to my business. He or she is not looking for immediate gratification and is willing to stay in treatment for the long run. The perfect client is enthusiastic, has good hygiene, gives feedback and is willing to learn lessons as a part of the healing process.

You may have more to add. By defining your perfect client, you are telling the universe who you want to have as a client. You will then attract that client and consequently end up with a more satisfying business. When you work with your Vision Declaration in the morning or evening, add a moment in which you visualize your perfect clients.

There might be a time when you attract a lot of "less than perfect" clients. This might indicate that it is time to redefine a part of your business/service or to clarify to clients what it is that you do. At this stage, you might need to look at what is going on in your life that is attracting this situation and address it, or you may need to detoxify your business and then realign with your definition of the perfect client.

Starters – Work through all the information in this chapter. Become aware of those areas within yourself that need to be strengthened. The more work you put into your vision, goals, and affirmations, the better your foundation will be. If your modality falls within the energy world, get as much experience as you can before you hang your shingle. There is a thought that you should receive money for your sessions. I believe, when you are new, you need a lot of experience. If you can offer your service for free for a few months, you will learn a lot about energy and how to talk about energy with your client. During this time you will develop rapport and get clarity on the type of business you want. Your trade is that you get experience and they get Reiki, healing touch or whatever modality you use.

Growers – Keep that list of goals going. A lot of times we step away from our list of goals and our energy gets fragmented and nothing gets done. What areas within your mind and emotions needs to be strengthened to support the direction you are going in? Make sure that you are getting coaching or work to align your mind and emotions around supporting you. Now that you have worked with clients, look at who your ideal clients are. Maybe it is time to redefine this.

Expanders – At this stage you might want to redo your vision. You are expanding or about to expand in new ways. How does that change your vision, goals and affirmations? Here are some questions to ask at this stage. What am I doing that could be improved? What have I been avoiding that needs to be done? Is it time to create a schedule of the hours you are available and not available? Many practitioners want to be available all the time and never have any time to themselves. What ideas have you thought of that you would like to implement but have not? What classes are you ready to teach or what classes would you like to take?

The expanders should take an afternoon a week and do nothing. This means no cleaning, running errands, or business. Two to four hours of quiet. I call this a strategic pause. Listen to your inner wisdom down as it speaks to you from the silence. You are creating space for this to happen. If you do not do this, you are blocking the flow of divine ideas that are here to guide you. Also this quiet space allows you to reenergize and find balance. Who wants to be worked on by a practitioner that looks like they are falling apart because of their own stress from over working or worry?

BUSINESS ENTITY AND BUSINESS PLAN

Business Entity

If you have not chosen what type of business entity to form, you have several options. I recommend that you discuss the pros and cons of each of these with an accountant or lawyer and find which one is most appropriate for what you plan to do.

Sole proprietorship means one owner. The owner assumes all responsibilities for the business, including assets and liabilities. Business income is taxed as personal income.

Some advantages of the sole proprietorship include less paperwork, minimal legal restrictions, owner retention of all profits, and ease in discontinuing the business. In most cases, a sole proprietorship is not required to obtain an Employer Identification Number (EIN) from the Internal Revenue Service unless it has employees.

There is no need to file a separate income tax return for the proprietorship because the activity is reported on the owner's federal and individual income tax returns. If you are a self-employed sole proprietor, you must make quarterly estimated payments to provide for these tax liabilities.

Disadvantages include unlimited personal liability for all debts and liabilities of the business, limited ability to raise capital, and termination of the business upon the owner's death.

General partnership lets two or more people share profits and liabilities. A general partnership is similar to a sole proprietorship, except that two or more parties are involved. In a business partnership, the parties that join forces could be individuals, corporations, trusts, other partnerships, or a combination of all of the above. The partnership is formed by an agreement entered into by each partner. It is advisable to have a written agreement drawn up between all parties.

Advantages are that it is easy to establish, can draw upon the financial and managerial strength of all the partners, and the profits are not directly taxed.

Some disadvantages are unlimited personal liability of the partners for the firm's debts and liabilities, termination of the business with the death of a partner (in the absence of advance planning for business continuation) and the fact that any one of the partners can commit the firm to obligations.

Limited Liability Company (LLC) is a hybrid between a partnership and a corporation, combining the limited liability advantage of a corporation with the tax status of a sole proprietor or partnership.

Similar to the partnership entities, the LLC is governed by an operating agreement. As a separate legal entity, LLC's may own property, sue, and be sued in the LLC's name. Unless otherwise specified by the Articles of Organization, LLC's enjoy perpetual continuity in the same way a corporation does. Since an LLC is a legal entity, the formation of an LLC requires more legal documentation than in a general partnership or sole proprietorship.

Corporation (C or S) is a state-chartered organization that acts as a separate legal entity and is the most structured business entity. Business activities are restricted to those listed in the corporate charter. Corporations may elect to file as a C-Corporation or S-Corporation. The differences are defined by the tax filing status as determined by the chapters in the Internal Revenue Code.

A *C-corporation* pays federal and state income taxes on earnings. When the earnings are distributed to the shareholders as dividends, the earnings are taxed again. Double taxation is a big drawback of C-corporations.

An S-corporation has the same legal attributes as C-corporations, but the corporation does not pay income taxes on earnings; instead, the shareholder pays income tax on dividends on their personal income tax return. S-corporations have fewer than 100 employees.

Liability is limited to the amount owners have paid into their share of stock, and the corporation's continuity is unaffected by the death or transfer of shares by any of the owners. Corporations have perpetual continuity unless otherwise specified in a Certificate of Incorporation. As a separate legal entity, corporations may own property, sue, and be sued in the corporate name. The disadvantages are extensive record keeping and close regulation.

After you have chosen the way in which you would like to operate, you will need to pick a name for your company. Naming the business is a critical step. You can select a business name and register it yourself, or you can hire a professional to do the search on availability and file the necessary forms. When you have selected a name, you can check to see whether or not it is being used by anyone else by contacting the appropriate state government office. After your name has been approved, you will need to register your company's name with your state government's taxation and assessment office or department of revenue. Your accountant should be able to direct you to the right government office. If you are forming an LLC or Corporation, you will need to file your Articles of Incorporation with the right appropriate state authority. After filing your Articles of Incorporation, you will need an Employee Identification Number (EIN). Your bank may not let you open a checking account for your business unless you have one. Here is the link on how to apply for an EIN from the IRS website https://www.irs.gov/businesses/small-businesses-self-employed/how-to-apply-for-an-ein.

Applying for an EIN is a free service offered by the Internal Revenue Service. Beware of websites on the Internet that charge for this free service.

Business Plan

For most companies seeking loans to start or expand their business, a well-written business plan is a necessity. In the field of holistic health, unless you need to borrow money from a bank, an in-depth business plan is not always necessary. It is a roadmap of what the business owner intends to do with the company and how he or she intends to make money and spend money over a specific time period (usually five years). If you are opening your own spa, holistic health center, or business that requires you to buy or rent a building, investing the time and energy to put together a comprehensive plan is a smart thing to do. If you are running your business out of your home with minimal expense, do not intend to borrow money for your business and are content with your business planning, you may want to skim this section and move to the next section. Just remember that if you decide to expand your business and borrow money, you might need a well-thought-out business plan.

The business plan should be written in a clear and concise manner. Whoever reads it needs to be able to understand what you do, how you do it, what your credentials are, and how you intend to make money. The fewer questions your soon-to-be creditors have, the better. As you write your plan, ask yourself whether you yourself would loan money for the venture you are outlining. When your plan is complete, you might want to solicit the opinions of others who will be very honest with you. You can get help from a member of Counselors to America's Small Business (SCORE) or the Small Business Association. There are many SCORE chapters across the country. SCORE members are retired businessmen and women who want to help small business owners to be successful. Look them up at www.score.org. You can also find many great books on the market that will help you through the process.

The many areas that are necessary for a business plan are:

The Executive Summary – describe the company history and objectives, your services and/or products, projected growth, why you will succeed, and the funding requirements.

The Products and Services – provide detail about your service, the need for it, what makes it unique and your competitive advantage.

The Market – provide statistics on market research data on the market demand for your service or product and indicate how much of that market you intend to capture.

The Marketing Strategy – discuss in detail the places you intend to market your services or products. Include samples of your current marketing materials that have been successful in generating business. Also include costs and information on how you will track the effectiveness of the marketing methods that you use.

The Competition – provide information on your competition, what makes you different from them, and the impact that their success will have on your business.

How You Manage Your Business – delineate the details of the qualifications of the key personnel and their roles.

Personnel – discuss how many people you will hire and the skills that they will need. Also include any considerations concerning pay, benefits, and overtime.

Financial Data – provide all the financial data necessary in order to show the loaning institution or individual how you plan to use the money and when you plan to make a profit. Documents that they will need are: the balance sheet, profit and loss statement and cash flow projections.

Financing Your Dream

Depending on what your vision is for your business, you may find that you need some form of financing to get it started or to expand it. You might take the traditional route and present your business plan to a bank in order to get a loan or a line of credit. You can also go to the Small Business Administration (SBA) with your completed business plan and be approved by the SBA for a loan that they guarantee, which makes it easier to get funding.

When you're considering ways to get financing for your business, it's important to think outside the box. You might seek a loan from supportive family members, consider a second mortgage or equity lines of credit on your home, find an investor, or take a loan on your 401K or retirement account. If you truly believe in yourself and the work that you do, then it should be easy for you to seek funding in these areas. If you receive money from someone outside your house equity or retirement account, make sure you have a lawyer draw up the paperwork for the agreement and that all parties read and sign it. Make sure that you are comfortable with the payment schedule and terms of the agreement before signing. And be sure to get the paperwork notarized. If you are going to have this person as a partner of some type, make sure those terms are delineated in a legal form and make sure that you are in agreement with how the business will be run, what will be bought to support it, and each person's roles and responsibilities.

You can also consider crowd funding. Crowd funding allows you to ask people to fund your business. You go through one of the online crowd funding sites and tell your story of how much money you need and what you are going to do with it. If people believe in your dream or feel connected to it, they give you the money. Most of the time, the person asking for the money promises something in return to those donating money, maybe a free session once you are up and running. These sites usually charge a fee of 5%. If a crowd funding site says free, read the small print. The most popular crowd funding sites are gofundme, kickstarter, indigogo, teespring, patreon, youcaring, crowdrise, kiva, and giveforward. Go to each site and read their rules and their fees.

Starters – Make your list of expenses so that you know up front what you need to get started. Decide what form of business you want to create. Look at the different areas of the business plan and go through an exercise of writing two to three paragraphs for each section. This is a valuable exercise in helping you to understand where you want to go and how you are going to get there. If you have questions about running a business, make an appointment at your local small business administration office. They offer free advice and classes.

Growers and Expanders – Define how much money you need to take the next steps. If your net income is over $20,000 a year, you might want to become an S-corporation. It will lower your amount of social security tax by half. You will only have to pay the corporation portion. If you are ready to move into a bigger space and know that you will need a loan, write a business plan. If you need help there are templates on the SCORE website. There are many templates online and a lot of great books that can tell you how to write a professional looking and sounding plan.

TAKING YOUR MESSAGE OUT TO THE WORLD

The Introduction

You offer a great service and have the training to back it up. Everyone you meet, no matter where life takes you, is a potential client or student. Say that you are out and about and meet someone new. You both begin talking about what you do. If it takes you a long time to make your point, you could lose his or her attention before you've acquired a new client.

Before you go out into the world to share your message with everyone you meet, you need a good, clear and concise introduction statement about who you are and what you do. You want your words to elicit interest. Do not fill your introduction with technical jargon or you will quickly lose your listener's attention. Always make sure you carry business cards to give out during your introduction. As you formulate your introduction, make sure you discuss a major benefit or two that your service provides. Use words that make it personal such as "**You** will **love** how **effective** acupuncture is in **reducing stress**," instead of "acupuncture reduces stress." You have an opportunity to make a good impression and to pique interest. It might be the only time you will meet this person, so make a positive impression.

Some people, for whatever reason, won't be interested in your introduction. Watch the person's body language for cues of whether he or she is interested. Know when to save your breath, and know when someone wants additional information about what you can do for them.

Think about how other people have introduced themselves and their work. What made the meeting memorable or impressionable?

Write down your introduction. Work with it by saying it out loud to make sure it sounds natural. Then shorten it and read it out loud again. You never know how much time you are really going to have. Memorize it at first so that you get the most important points out in your introduction. As you work with it over time, you will naturally become poised and comfortable with discussing what you do with just about anyone. Take time to write your intro down.

When you are comfortable with your introduction, practice it on your friends and family. Allow them to provide you honest feedback and then make the modifications necessary so that your introduction is perfect. Practice, practice, practice, until it sounds natural and you are comfortable.

Building Rapport and Trust

Establishing and building relationships with clients is necessary, but not always easy. In order to get clients to return for repeat services, it is crucial to establish rapport and trust. The client needs to feel comfortable with you as his/her practitioner, which means he/she needs to feel confident about your judgment and skills. Most importantly, you need to earn your clients' trust.

It takes time to build confidence and trust. To expedite that process you can practice active listening skills to hear your client's concerns and issues. That way the client feels respected and feels that you, the practitioner, are hearing their situation. You should then ask questions that help you to understand the client's situation more thoroughly and show that you really care. At the end of the first session, you should sit with the client and discuss a plan of action that is comfortable for the client.

It might be tempting to state the obvious to a client, to point out that he/she needs to lose weight, stop smoking, change his/her attitude or drastically alter his/her habits. Well, guess what? You won't be the first person—or the last—to give him/her such advice. He's/She's heard it all before and preaching to him/her may just stress him/her out and will not build rapport. I know that these issues are ones that need to be addressed. But you do not have to do it in a preachy way or shove it down their throat. You may want to find ways to help him/her to release the blocks to these issues before insisting that they stop these toxic habits. With this approach the client feels empowered to address the issues.

Helping him/her to establish a plan that he/she can live with and work with a step at a time will build rapport and trust. So don't propose the impossible on the first visit. Get to know the client, so that you can find solutions that work with his/her personality at his/her own speed until the client is ready to move forward. Some clients are ready to move quickly while others are only comfortable proceeding very slowly. You can assess the client's comfort level at the first couple of visits. Before your client leaves, schedule their next session; if you think one is warranted. Holistic health practitioners sometimes make the mistake of waiting for clients to reschedule. Sometimes they just need to be asked when they are available for the follow-up appointment.

Establishing rapport may begin with their first telephone call to you. Be attentive, sincere and listen. Clients can tell a lot about you from a phone call. Answer all questions that they might have and ask them if they would like to schedule a session. If the answer is "not at this time," thank them for calling and direct them to your website for more information. Tell them that you are available to answer any of their concerns or questions in the future. If they do schedule a session, you might want to write down a few relevant notes from your conversation. Your new client will be impressed that you remembered what he/she shared with you over the telephone when you meet.

Sometimes clients will express concern in an initial telephone call or at a first visit about the number of visits that might be necessary in order for them to experience relief or to heal. The first thing I tell clients is, "My goal is to work with you so that you no longer need to see me." If I have just completed a session with a client, I can then give him an estimate of the number of visits and can suggest how that might change over the course of treatment. If a client asks about the number of treatments in an initial phone call, I explain that I would need to see him/her in person for a session in order to be able to respond to that question. Honesty is always the best policy.

Building rapport is also about being in sync with your client. You might be all geared up from a great day of working with energy. Your client might arrive feeling very depleted and tired. Do not bowl him over with your whirlwind of energy by expecting him to be where you are. Greet him where he is at. It's not about lowering your energy, but about making the client feel comfortable. You may know some practitioners whose energy is so focused that it's almost laser-like. The intensity of such energy can be overwhelming and can feel like too much to handle.

At the end of each session, if needed, schedule your client's next session.

If you find that you're not getting the repeat business that you'd like, you might want to seek some feedback. Send your clients a letter and an evaluation form. Make sure they can fill it out anonymously and be sure to enclose a self-addressed stamped envelope to make it easy for them to return it to you. In the letter, tell them that you are seeking feedback on ways to improve your service to your clients and that you would love their views. Make sure the questions you include will provide the information that you need to help you improve your business. Limit the evaluation to about 20 questions and consider enclosing a 10% discount coupon to encourage responses to your questionnaire. You could also send out a survey via surveymonkey.com that lets those answering the survey fill it out anonymously.

Here are some tips to building rapport in person and on the telephone:

- Get their name and remember it. Use their name.

- Put yourself in their shoes. They are calling you because they have an issue. Be patient and listen as they share. Let them get it all out. For many clients that is why they are there. They just need to talk.
- Make sure you understand what is important to them. Repeat back to them their intention for the session. They will then begin to trust you.
- Do not make any assumptions. Always ask questions for clarity.
- Show your confidence and compassion.
- Match their tone, tempo, and volume if appropriate. This will make them comfortable.
- Have strong yet comforting body language.
- Do not rush your clients. They probably feel rushed in most of the other places of their life. Building rapport is important.
- Be mindful of your intonation. Go up at the end of your sentence for questions and down at the end of the sentence for giving direction or information.
- Be direct but not bossy.
- Be kind and smile a lot.
- Stay focused. Do not get side tracked by your cell phone or other people. Turn your cell phone off after your client arrives.
- Always show respect!

The bottom line is that treating your clients with sincerity and respect, along with formulating a plan of action that works *with* your client, will help to establish the foundation of a good client/practitioner relationship. You'll be guaranteed repeat business, and you'll likely receive some referrals from your satisfied clients.

The Talk

Every serious practitioner needs a half-hour or hour talk that educates potential clients and/or students. Being prepared with your talk provides you an opportunity to market your business and to educate a lot of people in a short amount of time. No matter what your field of expertise is, you need to be able to explain what it is that you do and *why* potential clients will benefit from your treatment. A talk performed well normally produces new clients or students. Most one-hour-long or shorter speaking opportunities are provided for free or for less than $100. The benefit for you is exposure to a group of people that you normally might not meet.

When presenting, start with a good introduction of who you are, your training, how long you have worked in the field, and any organizations that you are affiliated with that hold meaning for the audience you are addressing. Next, clearly explain what it is that you do and the benefits (why the audience needs to receive or learn what you do). Do not burden your listeners with a lot of esoteric jargon or you will lose their attention.

Keep the focus on your success stories and check your ego at the door; your audience can tell the difference between sharing and bragging. Share the examples that will be most meaningful to your particular audience. For example, if your audience is made up of breast cancer patients, focus on how your specific modality helps those with cancer.

Emphasize the benefits over and over again. Make sure the ideas that you are presenting flow smoothly. A focused and organized strategy will keep potential clients interested. Avoid complex ideas/theories, as many in your audience may be hearing for the first time about your area of expertise. You cannot afford to turn them off. Explain to them what a typical session is like, or let them know what to expect from your yoga class.

If you are new to making an hour presentation, ask your audience to hold all questions until the end, so that you won't get sidetracked and miss key points. Work from a good outline, but avoid reading from a script. An unrehearsed presentation or one where you are reading all of your notes, might give the impression that you're not well versed in your field. Provide visuals such as pictures, charts, or PowerPoint slides in order to hold your audience's attention. Too many visuals or ones that are overly detailed can be problematic, though, requiring a lengthy explanation of every element on your chart.

If you have time, demonstrate your skill. Make sure it fits into your time frame and allows you time at the end of your presentation to answer questions. Take questions when you finish making your points. If there are more questions and you've run out of time, offer to reconvene at another location nearby in order to have more time with the audience.

When making a presentation, pass around a sign-up sheet with a place for name, telephone number and email address. Collecting this information can be a vital tool in building your email list of potential clients/students. Provide each person with an article that you have written on the subject. If you have a flyer, brochure, or newsletter, make sure everyone gets a copy. Make sure that your name, telephone number, email address and webpage are included on everything you hand out. Business cards are fine, but the handouts suggested above will educate your clients after they leave your talk. You might also provide potential clients and/or students with a schedule of your current activities, as well as where they can find information on future events. Send them a follow-up email offering them a discounted session or give them a coupon at the talk for the same.

If you're one of the many people who find public speaking a challenge, my advice is to join your local Toastmasters group www.toastmasters.org. They offer great advice on how to give a speech. They also provide opportunities for members to give prepared speeches and short impromptu talks. You receive great feedback and have the opportunity to learn and gain confidence as you listen and watch other more experienced speakers. You could also take a speech class at your local community college in order to gain confidence and experience.

Participating in Conferences, Holistic Fairs and Festivals, and Other Venues.

These events provide holistic health practitioners with many opportunities for exposure to new clients and growth. Holistic Fairs can bring new clients as well as referrals. They can be a place to find strategic partners and other business enhancing opportunities, such as discovering new places to teach workshops or give talks. They are an opportunity to generate interest in your business.

When planning to attend one of these events, it is best to be organized, energized, and have a strategy together before you show up. You can use these events as a way to increase clientele, gain referrals, network and make possible business alliances. You can also learn by observing other vendors and holistic providers that are present.

The first thing to think about when considering an event is its proximity to your office. If it is more than an hour from your office, it is most likely too far to go to make it worth the fee you will pay to participate. If it is further away and you are inclined to attend, think about whether there are some additional business opportunities, such as hospital representatives being present who might be looking for therapists or if you are selling products sought out by the group attending. This might be worth your while.

If you can get a copy of the layout ahead of time, choose the space you want that would be ideal. You want to be located where the traffic is moving toward you, not hidden away in a corner. You also want to be located where there is not a lot of noise. You want to be able to hear and be heard when speaking with potential clients. If you do not like the location of your booth, then pull out or you will spend your time being miserable.

Ask the promoters of the event if you can give a short presentation. Most holistic health fairs have a room where presenters give talks to those attending the fair. Ask about this as soon as you find out about the event. These opportunities fill up quickly.

Preparing for the event is very important. Promote this event in advance. Tell everyone about the amazing event and how they will benefit from attending. Invite everyone. Tell them where they can find you at the event.

Make a list of everything that you will need considering how big a space that you will be getting. Ask yourself: Am I going to do sample treatments? How long? Am I going to charge money? Will the atmosphere lend itself for treatments? Is there room enough for a massage table or should I take a massage chair or just a chair to do energy work? What do I need to take for my table? How will I set myself up when doing sessions so that I generate interest? How do I want to get contact information from those interested? A signup sheet, a raffle for a free session, email addresses for a free newsletter, etc.

Here are some things to think about for your upcoming event:

- What type of material are you taking with you that your potential clients can take with them? Flyers, business cards, menu cards, or brochures. These should include your picture, phone number, web address and email address.
- Will you need electricity for your table? Make sure you get a setup that has access to electricity.
- Find out if you need to take a cover for the table that the organization is providing. Many times all of the tables have the same covering. Other times there is none and it is up to the participant to supply their own.

- Will you need to bring extra help? Someone to talk with the public while you are doing sessions. Someone to watch the table while you network and run to the restroom.
- What image do you want to give at this event? Is this event a professional conference or a spiritual festival? How will you fit in accordingly?
- Offer a giveaway by collecting emails for a prize to one or two people that day.
- Have a take away with your contact information on it, a pen, magnet, etc.
- Make your booth a destination. Have an eye catching sign to get them to come over to your display.
- What do you need for your safety and comfort as well as those attending?
- What dress is appropriate for the event?
- Will you offer demonstrations or have a video of your services on your tablet going the whole time.
- Your service may not be sought after by everyone. Focus on those who are showing an interest.

Here are some of the mistakes that participants make at these events:

- Wait for the opportunities to come to them.
- Play small or shy. Holding back will not make you the connections that you are seeking.
- Show up without being ready to talk about what they do or have the materials to give to potential clients.
- Talk too much without finding out what their potential clients are looking for.
- Have only their elevator speech ready. You need to be ready to dialog and appear to be seen as an expert in your field. Talk like one.
- Be too pushy.

After the event is over, what is your follow through plan of action? Enter emails into your email list. Send out emails thanking them for stopping by to meet you. Remind them of your services. Offer them a discount for their first service. Invite them to a free teleseminar. Follow up with an email a week later.

Starters – Begin working on developing good rapport. Perfect your introduction and practice it. Outline your hour talk. Practice it. Join Toastmasters.

Growers – Find places to offer your talk. Begin putting classes together to market at the end of your talks. Join Toastmasters.

Expanders – Find opportunities to be a keynote speaker at local conferences. Get your booth, spread your word. Make vital connections that will take your business to the next level.

MARKETING PLAN

Many holistic health providers are great practitioners of their modality, but they sometimes fall short in marketing their expertise. A practitioner I know had only one marketing tool—his business card—and yet he was mystified as to why he had not received more business. A marketing plan is an extremely useful tool. It will help you discern what your market is, what trends are occurring in that market, what strategies to use to increase your market share, and how to track the results. In terms of holistic health, you want to figure out who your potential clients are, how best to connect with them, and how to measure the results of the outcomes.

Even if you have the luxury of working in a spa or holistic healing center, it makes sense for you to learn marketing skills and begin learning how to market yourself. You might not always work for that center and that center may not always market to your particular clientele. Marketing is an integral part of a successful business, and it's never too soon to begin.

We've already reviewed a number of effective marketing strategies for increasing business. In the last chapter "Taking Your Message Out to the World," we discussed some basic marketing strategies. In the chapters that follow, additional marketing approaches and techniques will be offered. The better you understand your potential clients and how you can serve them, it will be easier to market your service effectively to them.

Marketing is a part of everything you do, from handing out business cards or pens with your number and logo, to placing a full-page advertisement in a local health-focused magazine. Before you begin marketing, decide how much money you want to invest and create a marketing budget. Business cards, brochures, postcard that list the menu of your services and free talks can be relatively inexpensive.

Placing advertisements, ordering signs, and social media advertising can be more expensive. A good mix of both can promote outstanding results. You will also need to have a method to track which marketing approaches generate clients or students. Tracking such information can be as simple as noting it on your client's intake form or more complex by linking google analytics to your website.

If you are new to the holistic health field or are not yet known as a practitioner in your area, an effective marketing plan will provide you a roadmap to ensure success. The bulk of your marketing expenses come in the initial outlay. As you begin to expand your business and receive referrals and repeat business, the expense for marketing your business will decrease.

As part of your marketing plan, list out your marketing costs including any software programs that are needed in marketing your services. If you are having brochures or business cards printed at local or online printers, get the costs. Knowing costs ahead of time, will keep you from being surprised by the total outlay that is needed.

YOUR WEBSITE

Every business needs a website. This is where most people go to find the services that they desire. Not many people use the Yellow Pages anymore. If you do not have a website, get one. You can design one yourself or have one designed for you by a website developer. Since I started my own business in 1992, before the Internet became popular, I have watched how creating a website has become easier and easier.

In the last year alone I have created two web/blog sites, check out www.energytransformations.org and www.heatrisingbook.com. I did the last one myself. There are several companies online that offer templates that will get you started with a basic website. They look good, are fairly inexpensive, and easy-to-use. Many companies like, Wordpress, offer free sites. In most cases if you want a specific domain name, you pay for your domain name and to register your website name. Your free site gives you blog pages, pages for "about your business page," and a contact page. In order to take payment on a website, you will need to pay for this ability.

If you do not want to build it yourself, you could also get a college student studying web design to build you a website at a discount or find a reputable person or company who can. Always get your login information that they are using. This way if they stop maintaining your site, you can give this information to the next person that will take over. Otherwise you are stuck having to pay someone to start the process all over again. Do not forget to change the website passwords if you switch web developers.

Having someone else build your site does not get you off the hook. You will need to provide the information/content about you, your services, your articles and products for the developer to place on your website.

In the online world, most of the time websites do not get a second chance. If they are boring or challenging to move through, your customer is gone very quickly. Think about how many websites exist on the Internet in your category of services offered. Make your site is one they want to explore. You want to make sure your website looks professional, is appealing to the eye, catches people's attention, and is easy to understand how to move through it. Have a domain name that is easy to remember and easy to spell. If you are processing payments on your site, you want to make sure your site is secured. Make sure the descriptions of what you do are to the point. Consumers move from website to website very quickly. Don't make them have to read a lot or make it hard for them to figure out what you do or you will lose them. Make sure your phone number is in a click and call format.

Here is some information that you want to include on your website:
- Your business name and an in-depth description of the services that you offer.
- Highlight what makes you or your services unique.
- A short biography and a description of what inspired you to start your business, including what motivated you to choose your field. This information can aid potential students or clients in deciding if you are the right fit for what they are seeking. List your credentials and awards.
- Articles that you have written describing your field of practice.
- Research data relating to your field of practice.
- Resource lists that would be helpful to students or clients.
- Articles written by you or your clients that discuss your successes.
- Testimonials.
- Information about each of the programs, workshops, retreats, speaking engagements, or free seminars you offer. Make sure you include dates, times, prices and let clients know how to sign up.
- How to set up an appointment with you.
- Directions to your location.

- Details of the products that you sell and information on how to order them.
- Promote any specials discounts.
- Contact information including your phone number and email address.
- Your newsletter.
- Information that tells the reader how to sign up for your newsletter and email list (this is important because it helps you to build your email list).
- Link all of the pages of your website with social media icons so that any or all of your information can be shared easily.
- Sign up boxes for visitors to sign up for your email list.
- Classes, workshops, retreats. Any events where you might be speaking.
- Any products that you sell.
- If you have an extensive website, make sure to offer a search capability or a sitemap to help people find what they are looking for.
- You might include a survey, if you want to collect a particular type of information from those visiting your site.
- Mention that you are offering free downloads of information in exchange for their email address.
- Create a blog or discussion group.
- Allow practitioners in other modalities to link with your site and make sure that you are linked with their sites. This helps your ranking in the search engine optimization.
- If you website becomes popular, you can sell advertisement space on your webpage.

There are so many online merchant services/sales carts available. A lot of businesses use PayPal. Square, along with Shopify, offer the same services along with a website to go with the payment taking process. You usually pay a monthly fee or pay less by paying yearly. After somebody pays for something on your site, you are notified via email of the sale. The money shows up in your bank account usually within two days.

The ideas listed above are only a starting point to build success by using your website. Visit other websites to get ideas. Go online and search "What makes a good website?" Make sure you use wording that the general public will understand.

The next time you're surfing the Internet, visit some websites that you find appealing and easy to use. What appealed to you? What did you learn? How can you apply what you liked to your website? How does this inspire you to relay your services and classes in an appealing manner?

Grow Your Business Using the Internet

The Internet has forums where you can establish meet up groups for people in your area with the same interests. Go on Meetup.com and look to see if there are any groups in your area that you are interested in. Join them. Offer to present to the group. Use the groups to network. Make friends and learn. Yahoo Groups are discussion groups. Each group focuses on specific areas. Search on Yahoo Groups so you see the variety of groups offered. When you join a group, you get the information in your email and can post to the groups as well.

The Internet also contains names and information about organizations that would benefit from your presentation. You can look up your local support groups, hospitals, and community organizations on the Internet and find a telephone number or email address.

The Internet can also be used for research. If you are working on an article or paper, you can find a wealth of information online and you can also connect to people in your field who have already blazed a trail.

In order to maximize the Internet's potential to support your business, build your email lists! Make sure you get an email address from each of your clients or students. When you do talks, collect names and email addresses. Emailing allows you to get your message out to a lot of people at once, and it saves you the time and money that it costs to mail out postcards or flyers. Of course, it's important to use the Internet wisely: no one wants to be inundated with emails reminding them of services or suggesting new appointments. But if it's used judiciously, your email address list will help you keep in contact with your clients and keep them up to date on specials or workshops. Make sure to include your website address in each email. When recipients of your email forward it to others, anyone who wants to know more about your business can contact you easily.

The next time you're surfing the Internet, visit some websites that you find appealing and easy to use. What appealed to you? What did you learn? How can you apply what you liked to your website? How does this inspire you to advertise/display your services and classes in an appealing manner?

Another way to generate income from your website is to use Goggle Ad Sense or the yahoo equivalent found under Search Marketing. These campaigns allow you to earn money for letting Google or Yahoo display relevant ads on your website's content pages. These ads are related to what your visitors are looking for on your site.

Other types of Internet advertising that you might want to explore include:
- Text ads
- Pop ups
- Banners
- Paid Listings in Directories
- Free Listings in Directories
- Your weblink listed on other websites

Aside from your website, the Internet offers opportunities for you to list your name in directories for your field of expertise. Check the various websites that offer directories of Holistic Health Practitioners and make sure you are on these lists. People seeking practitioners in these fields visit these directories to find someone close to where they live or work to get a treatment. Some websites let you list your business for free while others require you to pay a small fee. Before you sign up for a paid listing, review the site and see if it meets your standard of professional design and content. There are many directories on the web and many list practitioners from various modalities.

Exercise 2: Exploring the Internet – Go online. Begin gathering information to use for setting up your own website or improving your existing site. Look at other websites and notice what you like or do not like about them. Add your name to some directories related to your field. Begin building or expanding your email address list. Develop a newsletter that you can send out to your email list. Make sure the information in it is something your readers will enjoy.

The World of Technology

The world has come a long way in technology since I started my Reiki business. A lot of holistic practitioners do much of their business using their phones, i.e. scheduling appointments, texting clients, uploading information to social media, and using the camera on their phones to make a video. There are so many free apps that you can download to support your business. Ask around to see what people are using and why they like it. If it makes your life easier, why not use it?

Technology has made it so much easier to do just about anything that you can imagine. I recently created an online class using another business' frontend for the class. All I had to do was to develop the material and upload it to their site. With my computer, I could record video and audio. I did buy a Blue Yeti™ microphone that plugged into my computer, which produced better sound. I was able to create PowerPoints™ and turn them into videos, record meditations for my lessons on my computer and mix the voice with music, as well as create short videos. In the past, I would have had to go to a studio to do all of this and pay a big price.

What do you want to create to take your business to the next level? What technology will you need? Think big and go for it!

Starters – Build your website. Get your friends and family to use it and to give your feedback.

Growers – Make it possible for your clients to schedule their session on your website and pay for it there as well. Link your website with other sites.

Expanders – What products can you sell on your website? Make sure you are blogging on your website. By consistently putting new material on your website, your site shows up higher in search engine searches on your subject area.

MARKETING ON THE INTERNET AND SOCIAL MEDIA

Since I began my part-time Reiki business in 1993, the Internet has come of age and social media is taking us to the next level of connecting with potential clients around the globe. If you are a life coach, this has opened up new ways for you to connect with prospective clients. For energy workers, massage therapists, acupuncturist(s) and the like, social media might not help you as much. I offer distant Reiki sessions, so social media has helped a bit. But for those of you that take clients locally, getting out in the public, giving talks in your community, and networking might just be time that is better spent than being on social media.

If you are going to get on social media, use it to build a positive reputation in your field. Share your successes without giving away too many details or your clients' names. Ask them permission before you post anything. You never know who will look at your post and have a relative that lives nearby that could benefit from your service.

To start or grow any business, face to face meetings are the best and least expensive marketing that you can do. These people live in the same state and town that you do. This is not necessarily the case when you are meeting someone online. If I am starting a business, I would make it a priority to meet new people every day and spend less time on social media. But I know you want to engage on the Internet and social media so let's talk about how to do this well.

Here are some things that you might want to consider to get a broader exposure and potential material for your website:

- be a guest on someone's podcast/Internet radio show
- host your own podcast

- be a guest on someone's Internet television show
- host your own Internet television show
- upload your quality and interesting videos to YouTube™
- start a blog
- post on Facebook™
- post on Instagram™
- use Pinterest™
- be a guest blogger on someone else's blog site
- comment on topics in Reddit™ and Quora™
- join LinkedIn™
- join Alignable™

Podcasts/Internet Radio, Internet Television and YouTube

There are a plethora of podcasts. Find podcasts that draw the audience that would most likely be your potential clients. Propose a topic that you could present to the show host, via email. Most podcast hosts will ask you for your bio, a picture and information on the topic you will speak about. This information will be posted on their site. After the show is aired, go to the podcast site, download the interview file and put the recording on your website. It will make you look more like an expert in your area of expertise. Some podcasts will charge their guests a fee for having them on their show; others will not. The podcast host can put their shows on iTunes, Tunecore and many other sites that host audio and video productions.

I co-hosted a podcast show called Two Modern Mystics for two years. We did two shows a month from September through May. It was fun and exciting. We had some shows where my co-host and I would discuss topics such as forgiveness, acceptance, Reiki, etc. We also had shows where we interviewed various professionals that had a message that we liked. We loved what we did; however, it was a lot of work pulling all the information together. We were not as focused on using it to amp up our business, but more to connect our message to the world. It built my email list slightly.

In order to host the show we paid a fee, which can be paid monthly or annually. There were a variety of levels of service that you can buy into. Each level came with more capacity and more frills. You would have to decide what you want and need. If I were to do it again, I would make sure we included commercials for services and had more of a push to have giveaways for getting people to sign up for my newsletter.

Internet television seems to be the latest avenue of connecting. Even though YouTube has been around for a while and is expanding its arena, Internet television offers hosts their own show or a platform that is the front end to an audience. One of my friends has a show on a women's Internet television network. She used to have a podcast show focused on Reiki, with listeners from around the world. From what I was told, the expenses for the Internet television shows are a lot higher than podcast shows. She charges her guests a fee so that she can recoup her expenses.

With each adventure that you delve into there is a learning curve. We had to learn how to record the shows, upload information about each show on the website, troubleshoot issues, and tell our guests how to connect. We had to do the shows over a landline as it is more reliable than the wireless connections when recording using a cell phone. I am sure with an Internet television show there is even more to learn.

With both the podcasts and Internet television, the sites have all the statistics regarding how many people tuned in while you recorded, how many people listened in each day, and how long they stay listening or watching your show. The podcast provider also kept a count on how many people in total had watched each show. It was fun to see that people were listening when we were live and how many people listened to it after it was recorded. At first our numbers were low, but over time, as listeners found us they would listen to more than just the one show. By the time we started our second recording season our numbers made us very happy. Some podcast and Internet television stations will promote your shows depending on what package you purchased. What you need to remember is that they have a lot of shows to promote, so you need to be promoting your shows on your website and in social media as well.

Launched in May 2005, YouTube allows billions of people to discover, watch and share originally-created videos. YouTube provides a forum for people to connect, inform, and inspire others across the globe and it acts as a distribution platform for original content creators and advertisers large and small. YouTube offers you a place to put your videos out on the Internet. They do not promote your videos. If they are done well and have titles with good key words in them, they might just be found. If your videos are of great interest to the public then they might even go viral and you could become an Internet success overnight. You can make videos using your phone, your computer, a compact camera, a video camera and a good digital camera. There are free video editing software on most computers as well. All the details that you need are on YouTube's website. Get filming.

With any of these avenues, it is important to have titles for your shows that will show up well in the search engines. Make sure you use key words that people are looking for in your title so that your show is found by people putting words into the search engines. Just remember that all of these options involve taking time to learn the technical aspects as well as the time to prepare a good show. If you are just starting your business, put this on the back burner, unless you are showing up as a guest on someone else's show.

Blogging

Most website formats now allow you to have a blog on your site. Your blog is a way to connect with your clients and potential clients. Blog postings are usually around 350 to 600 words. Today's consumer does not stay on websites for a long period of time. Make your articles interesting and to the point. Have your contact information at the bottom of the article as well as all over your website. Make sure you include the social media share icons with your article so that someone can hit a button and your article is on Facebook or some other forum. The possibilities are endless. Make sure your menu across the top of the page has a link to your services and products. Make it easy to find the link to buying your services. If it is too hard, they move on to another webpage.

Once you have a strong blog of your own, offer to be a guest blogger on a fellow blogger's site. Make sure your topics of conversation relate. It could be a great way to get exposed to an audience that has never heard about you.

If your message is popular, people will begin following you. One blogger, the Crafty Chica, started blogging because she loved making crafts. She blogged about her projects, posted pictures and became an Internet success. I met Kathy Cano-Murillo when she spoke to my women's writers group. She went from writing a column in the newspaper to starting her own blog. It took off. She now has a product line at Michael's craft store, has taught art on cruise ships, gets paid to talk about what she loves doing, has written several craft books and continues doing what she loves.

Facebook/Instagram/Pinterest/Twitter

By all means get on Facebook. There are millions of people around the world on Facebook. Join Facebook groups related to your profession. Comment on posts. Give people a chance to get to know you. Do not post comments that are fear-filled, dramatic, or negative. These do not attract followers or new clients.

In the event section, list all of your upcoming events, classes, and retreats and post them so that they are open to the public. Ask your friends to share the information on your events with their friends. Do not post a ton of cute pictures or reposting things that are interesting to you. Many people are turned off by someone clogging up their view with crazy videos and old news that has been posted over and over again. If you do this, you risk being unfriended or your posts being ignored.

Make a business Facebook page for your business. Make it look professional. Make sure you include an email address where prospective clients can get a hold of you. I would not post a phone number or who knows how many strange phone calls you would get.

Instagram is a community of more than 500 million who capture and share the world's moments on the service. Instagram has become the home for visual storytelling for everyone from celebrities, newsrooms and brands, to teens, musicians and anyone with a creative passion. I do not see how Instagram can do a lot for a holistic business. If you use this, you should have clever images that can portray the point that you want to get across to get followers.

Pinterest is a free website where users can upload, save, sort, and manage images—known as pins—and other media content (e.g., videos) through collections known as pinboards. Pinterest acts as a personalized media platform. Users can browse the content of others in their feed. Users can then save individual pins to one of their own boards using the "Pin It" button, with pinboards typically organized by a central topic or theme. Users can personalize their experience by pinning items, creating boards, and interacting with other members. The end result is that the "pin feed" of each user displays unique, personalized results. As of December 2016, Pinterest had 150 million active users.

I am not sure how Twitter can help you to build a holistic business or expand one. If you are a life coach, I would consider Twitter. If you provide other services, it might serve you to wait until you are well known before you take time to tweet. Twitter is a place to microblog your thoughts, getting your message out to the people that follow you using only 140 characters. As of February 2017, 319 million people are active on Twitter. If you do use Twitter or Instagram, remember to use the appropriate hashtags as these are the terms the users are searching to find what interests them.

With all social media do not spend your whole day on your computer or your phone. Most of your clients are not in the Internet world, they are the people in your community, town, county and state. Social media should be used as a platform to highlight your professionalism, caring, and skillset to attract potential clients. I would not spend more than 15-30 minutes a day on social media. If you are building a business or have a successful business, it is because you know how to manage your time in other areas that are more important.

Reddit and Quora

Reddit is a website to post conversations, articles, questions and have a discussion. Reddit's registered community members can submit content, such as text posts or direct links. Registered users can then vote submissions up or down to organize the posts and determine their position on the site's pages. The submissions with the most positive votes appear on the front page or the top of a category. Content entries are organized by areas of interest called "subreddits". The subreddit topics include news, science, gaming, movies, music, books, fitness, Reiki, spirituality, consciousness, and image-sharing, among many others. Reddit averages about 542 million monthly visitors. Anyone can post or respond to other people's posts.

Quora is a question-and-answer site where questions are asked, answered, edited and organized by its community of users. It is a way to learn and to exchange information and ideas. Quora has about 100 million monthly visitors to its site.

Reddit and Quora are ways to network and build your reputation in the online community forums. It is good if you have the time.

Linkedin

LinkedIn is a social network for professionals. Whether you're a marketing executive at a major company, a business owner who runs a small local shop or even a first year college student looking to explore future career options, LinkedIn is a place you might find new opportunities to grow business. I was involved there for a few years and did not get any clients from it. My Linkedin id was taken over and I reported it and dropped out. I think Life Coaches might do well on LinkedIn. LinkedIn offers members a profile page, as well as opportunities to join groups and to send message. Most of the people that I know in the field of holistic health have dropped out of LinkedIn because they do not have the time to spend in online networks that do not help them to build their business.

Alignable

Another social network that I believe will work better for you than LInkedin is Alignable. Alignable is similar to Linkedin, but it is for your specific town/city. Alignable is free and allows you to enter a business profile so that other business owners in the network can find you. The website is www.alignable.com. After you join, they introduce your business to the other businesses in your area.

Build Your Email List

I can't say this enough, "Build your email list!" The success of a small business is ease of communication with your clients and to get new clients or information to contact possible new clients. The best way to do this is to build your email list and keep it up to date. There are a couple ways to build your list.

On all of your website pages, have a box where people can sign up for your newsletter. This means you need to commit to some type of newsletter emailing. If a newsletter is not your thing right away, you can have an email sign up box, by offering to give something free away in exchange for their name and email address. It could be a tips sheet on "how to" improve some aspect of their life, a free mp3 download of a meditation or a talk, a free sample of something you sell. You post the free download hidden on your website and when they sign up, the email they receive provides the link to the information. What you are offering to them has to be something that your target audience needs. What problem are you solving with your giveaway? Will what you have be enticing enough to get them to sign up?

There are several opt in tool forms available. Some are free and some charge a monthly fee. Here are a few: Lead Pages, Magic Action Box, Opt in Monster, and Sumome. If you know someone that does coding, they can add the code to your site to create the sign up boxes. Have these boxes on your blog pages and your product and services pages as well. To entice them to sign up, you want to have a clever box that says what your free offer is.

Offer a free teleseminar using one of the free teleconference services. This gets you emails. In order for them to get the number to call into the teleseminar, they need to sign up and give you their email address.

Have a sign-up sheet that collects names and email addresses when you go to any event. Maybe you are offering free mini Reiki or massage sessions at an event. Have them give you their information. Follow this up with an email with a coupon for a percentage off of their first service with you.

On your signature line on your emails, add a line that says sign up for my newsletter and receive your free (whatever it is you are offering) and add the link right there for them to click it within your email.

Once you have their emails, you can let them know what events, classes, or monthly specials you have going. When your email lists gets into the 100's you might want to consider an email marketing company. This allows you to upload your email lists and send out emails to your whole list without having your email provider shut you down. At one point my email list was 7,200. With my local Internet provider, it would take me up to two weeks to send out my newsletter. My email provider only allowed me to send out emails with up to 90 addresses and only 7 a day, spread out over the day. Otherwise, I would be flagged as spamming people and my email account would be closed.

Email marketing companies have free options for small lists. The benefit to using them is that they have great templates, have social media icons for sharing your email to social media platforms, and provide help along the way. I have worked with two of these companies and there were pros with both and not many cons, and my email goes out to my whole list all at one time.

Host an Online Class

The Internet has made it easy to host online trainings, summits, conferences, mini-talks, coaching sessions, or meetings. You can do this using your phone in the format of a teleconference, or you can do this from your computer using conferencing software which enables you to see the other people in the class. Skype, Zoom, and GotoMeeting provides the user the ability to connect with many people all at once. It allows desktop sharing of information such as documents, PowerPoints, and videos. You talk with each other face to face in real time. Most of these services charge a monthly fee.

Make Amazing Graphics

In this Internet age, graphics are what catch people's attention. I have been using Microsoft Publisher for many years. I can put together the most amazing images using this program. If you are a business owner, you should invest in Microsoft Office. It has a lot of the programs that you would need for your business.

Google Drive offers free programs similar to Microsoft Office. The web-based nature of Google Drive can be advantageous, but it can also create problems. If you lose connection to the Internet, you cannot edit your files. The web applications in Google Drive have enough features for basic use but do not have the full complexity of Microsoft Office.

Canva is a website where you can create graphics, documents, and designs that will give your website and social media posts the wow that you want. Canva has free and paid options as well.

Finding images to use is very easy. There are many websites with photos that you can pay for that are relatively inexpensive. Pexels.com and Pixabay.com offer images for free. They ask that you give credit to the photographer.

Remember, if you want to get a potential client's attention, your images need to look professional and appealing to grab their attention. Look at your website, social media pages, and blogs. Do you have amazing images there? If not, start uploading. Any image that you post on the Internet, other than your website, needs to have a link embedded it in that takes the viewers to your website or blogsite.

Paid Marketing on Social Media

This is a whole arena in itself. I have only begun exploring in this area. If you do not do it right, you waste a lot of money. Many people are gaining business from paid ads on social media marketing. If you do this right, you can build your email list, make sales and grow your business. Udemy.com has a few inexpensive online courses that teach how to maneuver through paid marketing on the social media sites.

You have to determine whether or social media marketing makes sense to grow a business that relies primarily on people that live close by that come to your office, not unless you do business via distance healing or Skype or other online video connecting services.

Facebook allows you to target your advertising down to the town/city you live in, male or female, and offers you age ranges of your target audience. You might want to test it out to see if it brings you new clients. Advertising starts at $5 a day.

NextDoor and Thumbtack

Nextdoor and Thumbtack are two good ways to grow and expand your business. Nextdoor.com is a social networking service for neighborhoods. It was launched in the United States in October 2011. Nextdoor allows users to connect with people who live in their own and nearby neighborhoods. Here is how you can use it.

First you have to go the website and sign up. It is free. Once your community verifies that you do live in the area, you will be allowed to post messages to the other people that live in your area and the surrounding communities.

Your first post to the group basically introduces who you are to the community. So you can say who you are and what you do. Then post your services in the classified section. You can ask your neighbors that receive a service to give you a shout out with a post saying how great you were. A lot of times, community members will post a question, such as what massage therapists would members recommend in the area. This is when you get on there and offer a discount for that person's first service with you.

There is also a place on NextDoor where businesses can have a listing. Get your business listed.

Thumbtack.com is a website that anyone with a legitimate business can sign up to participate in. Consumers use this website to find businesses that they are interested in. So if someone is looking for Reiki, they go into Thumbtack and ask for quotes from Reiki practitioners that work in their area. The person receives five quotes and the links to each responder's contact information. The practitioners responding are charged a fee for responding. The fee is very reasonable. Those receiving your service through Thumbtack have the opportunity to leave testimonials. There are several services that people ask for quotes where the services can be done from a distance. These services are life coaching, hypnotherapy, spiritual counseling, and card readings. This is a great way to build your business without anyone coming to your office.

Starters – Announce your services on social media. Let people know how skilled you are and how passionate about what you do. Offer a discount to get people in your door. Get on Nextdoor.com. Begin building your email list.

Growers – Continue to build your email list. Make sure your events are on Facebook's events page. Make a video about your services for your website. Start a blog and continue to blog. If it would help to grow your business, get on a local based Internet radio/podcast show.

Expanders – Make several videos. Get them up on your site and on YouTube. Host an online class. Host a summit. Think outside the box regarding ways you can use social media to expand your business.

PAPER-DRIVEN MARKETING

In this section we will review the "paper-driven" approach to marketing your business. Whatever medium you choose to relay your message, make sure you spell check and have someone who is good at editing check all your publications before sending them out to the public. Typos or errors could end up costing you money. Take extra care in making sure your fee structure is listed correctly. Wherever you decide to place your business cards, flyers or brochures, visit those locations periodically to drop off new materials and to see how they are being displayed.

Business Cards

A good business card is essential. Of course you'll include the basics on your card – your name, telephone number and email address and website. Be careful about overloading the card with too much information. You can make one yourself or have it professionally made. Microsoft Publisher is an easy to use software for making all types of business cards, flyers and brochures. Many office supply stores sell business card paper that does not leave notches on the sides of your cards. Making your own cards gives you the option to change the design or wording anytime and to print as many as you need. Name changes, email address or phone number changes are easy to take care of when you print up cards yourself. You can also load your files onto the online printing stores such as VistaPrint and others and get a very professional looking card that you designed.

Make sure your card is appealing. Use a balanced design and a font that is easy to read. Distinctive business cards include one or more of the following:

- a unique symbol
- raised print that adds a textured dynamic
- a combination of dark and light color contrasts
- catchy or interesting mottos
- interesting background scenes
- concise wording that describes the service or product

Having cards professionally designed or printed usually provides you many more design options. They might cost more, but you'll end up with a more sophisticated look. It's worth it to demonstrate to your potential clients that you are serious about business. If you have cards printed professionally, you usually have to purchase at least 500 or 1000 at a time.

Most online business card printers offer you an electronic version of your business card that you can put on your emails or other electronic communications or website. Most of these online businesses also offer printing of brochures, post cards, flyers, and promotional items such as magnets and bookmarks. They also make signs and banners. They have a variety of templates and images for your marketing material.

Flyers

When I started my part-time holistic business, flyers were a popular way to advertise services and workshops. However, in today's world I see lots of business cards and not many flyers or brochures in public places.

If you do have places to use your flyers, consider the following when you create them: Think about who your target audience is. Are they medical personnel? If so, make sure your wording would draw their interest. A flyer for this audience would be a lot different than one for the general population. If you are using the flyer for your services, make sure you include the benefits that clients will receive in using your service. This flyer might be your first impression, so make it a good one. Make sure your contact information is on the flyer as well as the correct dates for any event you are advertising.

Flyers are typically easy to put together; the paper is relatively inexpensive and the template for some classes only requires that dates and times be changed.

The flyers that turn people off are ones that have been copied over and over again. The print might be faded or illegible in spots. Or the text might be off center or misaligned. Your flyer should reflect the same attention to detail that you maintain in the other aspects of your business. As a rule, use 8 ½ x 11 paper, select a color that matches the theme and will attract attention in a positive way. Limit yourself to one or two fonts throughout, allow ¾-inch margins on all sides, and run your spell checker.

Brochures

Brochures are very appealing to the public. The design layout and space allows you to catch someone's attention while providing them information about you and your service. You can lay out a brochure on your home computer using publishing software or have them created professionally. The difference is the time and expense. Professionally made brochures cost a lot more and you still have to create the text and think through the look you want. So why not do it yourself?

Brochures can be used as both a marketing and an education tool. You can use the space to explain the *what, how,* and *why* of what you do. The information might inspire the reader to seek you out to ask more questions about your modality or to schedule an appointment. Make sure you make it easy for prospective clients to find your contact information on the brochure, so consider using a bold font. Tri-fold or quad-fold brochures work well because they fit into a #10 envelope.

Make sure your margins are equal. Select glossy paper for high profile and be sure to review before printing.

The information on the brochure is about your service, classes, and you. Avoid time-sensitive information like dates for workshops because it might make your brochures appear outdated. Place your brochures in doctors' offices and other professional settings. Make sure your brochure reads well, is not too technical, and includes the benefits your services provide, as well as information on how to contact you.

Menu Cards

I have seen a lot of post card style menu cards recently being used for marketing. Menu cards typically have the name of the company or therapists name, a list of their services, website, and contact information. If done with a postcard, the size is 3.5 inches x 5 inches. I have seen the menu cards as big as 6 inches by 9 inches. The one that I use is on the next page. I put it on my Google business page and have made copies of it to give to clients to give to others. You can also have it printed on a thicker material and have it framed in your office or sitting up on its own on a table. You subliminally plant the seeds, spelling out all that you have to offer. Clients might even ask questions about the services that are new to them, wondering if it could benefit them.

Energy Transformations

By appointment only

Menu of Services

- Reiki
- Life Coaching
- Distance Reiki
- Cord Cutting
- Sound Therapy
- Medical Intuitive Session
- Fertility Energy Assessments
- Wedding Officiant
- Reiki classes

http://www.energytransformations.org

phone number here

Placing Advertisements and Marketing Your Business

Advertising your business is important. Many practitioners expect that word of mouth and referrals will build a viable moneymaking practice, but it's important to get the word out to a larger audience about the services that you offer. Carefully and strategically placed ads can help to build your business. After you have your business up and running, you may find that you do not need to advertise as much as you did at the beginning.

Placing advertisements has its pluses and minuses. First, advertising gets your message out to a lot of people you would not normally meet. Written well, these ads can generate business. If you are advertising a class, getting one or two students from the ad would more than pay for it. All the rest of the attendees just add to your profit margin. But the drawback of advertising is that it tends to be expensive. Some cheaper venues include advertising in your community newsletter, or local health newsletter or specialty newsletter for men or women.

For me, the upfront work is finding out about the newsletter's or magazine's audience so that I can determine whether I want to place my ad. Does the publication get distributed to people who live in my area or up to an hour's drive from my business or workshop location? Are the readers those that would benefit by or be interested in my services? You might try contacting businesses that are similar to yours which have already placed ads in a publication that you are considering advertising in and ask if the investment was worth it. This could save you a lot of money.

Business-card-sized ads usually do not allow enough room for what I want to relay. Such small ads are easily overlooked by readers. Buy at least a quarter-page ad to draw more attention and to be able to include the main points. Make sure all of your pertinent contact information is in your ad, including your website. Be aware that some advertisers require that you send the ad in an electronic format such as a .pdf file or jpeg for format. Always ask if there are any discounts for a first time ad or for repeat ads.

Personally, I would start with your neighborhood newsletter. These are the people that live close by and could be potential clients. My neighbor is a massage therapist. When she moved her business into her home, she needed to grow her business all over again. She put a full page ad in her neighborhood newsletter. She introduced herself and her services, listing out the four forms of massage that she offered with her contact information. At the bottom of the page she offered a coupon for new clients that paid for a session. They would get a free session on their second visit or they could give the free session to a friend. Her business filled. After a few years she was trained in two additional areas. Again she took out a full page ad highlighting her new services as well as listing her other services. The coupon this time said, "Try one of my new services and get 50% off." She shared that her learning was to make sure you have an expiration date on the coupon.

Other than magazines and newspapers, you can advertise in the coupon circulars that are delivered in the mail. Including a discount coupon in a mass mailing may generate new business. I do not know many people that have grown their business this way. You may want to find a coupon for a business like yours and call them to ask how the service has worked to grow their business.

Another advertising avenue is purchasing a magnetic sign to place on your car. Wherever you go, your advertisement goes with you. If you try this approach, make sure your contact information is large enough for other drivers and pedestrians to see.

Exercise 3: Collect 10 business cards and critique them. What do you like about them, what grabs your attention, what detracts from them, what information is important and what is unimportant?

Exercise 4: Create a business card.

Exercise 5: Create a flyer for your business or class. List at least 10 places within a 40-minute drive from your office to place them.

Exercise 6: Look through several health/wellness related papers/journals and study the advertisements. See what grabs your attention. Create a quarter-page business ad 3 inches by 5 inches.

Exercise 7: Where can you advertise your services? Call several potential places and find out what the costs are to advertise.

Writing Articles for Newsletters, Newspapers and Magazines

One of the most effective ways to generate new clients and students is by publishing an article about your modality. Your article is an important educational tool and it can also give you credibility. Publishing an article allows you to educate your reading audience, tell the world about your skill, and let clients know how they can learn more and/or how to go about receiving a treatment. A well-written article has the potential to produce a lot of interested clients. Have someone who is unfamiliar with what you do read your article and provide feedback before you send it to a publisher. You don't want your article to sound like a sales pitch—most newspapers and magazines will warn you against that. At the end of the article, you are permitted to provide your name and maybe a phone number, email address, or website. Most of the time, the publication will offer you advertising space at a discount. Place an ad to provide any points or contact information that was not included in the article.

You can take a number of different angles with the article. You can just be informative or educational, explaining what your modality is and how it works. You can tell a particular success story or relate some facts about research that has been done in your area of practice. With this approach, be sure to cite the authority who did the research. A fourth angle is to tell how your modality works successfully for a specific condition. Whatever approach you choose, make sure that it is appealing and appropriate for the audience that will read it and do not sound like an advertisement.

When writing any article, think about what problem your potential client might have. Answer how can your modality offer relief or solve their issues? Then end your article with a call to action. Give them good information. Do not sound like an advertisement.

I can't stress enough how important it is to write for your audience. If you want to attract medical personnel to attend your workshop or receive a treatment, an article in a nurses' newsletter would bring you nurses. However, the article would need to focus on the benefits that they would get from receiving a treatment or from learning your skill. You would need to provide examples of how your skill is currently being used in the field or how your treatment helps nurses reduce personal stress. If you were writing an article for expectant mothers, the focus and information would be very different. I have written articles in journals for nurses, massage therapists, occupational therapists, medical personnel, and women, as well as for the general public. Most of the time I start fresh by focusing on the magazine's intended audience.

Any articles that you write, consider adding them to your blog. Use the material in as many different ways and as often as you can.

Exercise 8: Write down at least three potential places that you could have the article published. Contact a local paper and ask about submitting an article. Find out what their requirements are.

Exercise 9: Pick an intended audience and write an article about your service or workshop that is informative or tells a success story. Your article should be at least 300 to 750 words. Have someone read it and give you feedback.

A Newsletter

Your own newsletter is a great marketing tool for staying in contact with your clients and students. It can be one or several pages. Just make sure it is interesting and something people will want to read. In a newsletter you can educate your clients about the benefits you provide. You can share success stories. If you have a client who has a success to report, ask him or her to write an article for your newsletter. You can also post specials that you are having and provide dates for workshops.

I used to do a print newsletter that had to be mailed to over 700 people. It was a lot of work and expensive to print and to mail! Now I email my newsletter to 2,500 people and the list continues to grow. I also sell space for classified ads in the newsletter. It is an easy way to stay in touch with a lot of people. You can remind your clients and students to call and make an appointment or to sign up for the next workshop. Make sure your web address and telephone number are in your newsletter. Direct your clients to your website where they'll find lots more information. Your newsletter and website work hand in hand as valuable marketing tools. Make sure you have social media icons so that it is easy to share your newsletter articles with Facebook, Twitter, Instagram, etc.

Setting Your Message Apart from Your Peers

Strong creative writing skills are a must when it comes to marketing your service or product. Avoid making promises you can't keep and always be credible and honest. Use active words that get potential clients hopeful and excited about what you offer. In order to guarantee a successful response by consumers of holistic health services, you need to set yourself apart from other practitioners and therapists who offer the same service. If you do not distinguish yourself from others in your field, the general public will choose a service provider based on price, convenience, word of mouth or reputation, or personal relationships. Your marketing literature must convey a perceptible difference to attract potential clients.

Begin reading the advertising material published by practitioners and therapists in your field. What stands out? What appealed to you?

What turned you off? What seemed over the top? Read how others describe the benefits and services that they offer. You might also attend holistic health fairs to visit booths and listen to how therapists and practitioners describe the services that they offer. Visit holistic health websites and observe the buzzwords that work and those that do not. What colors schemes or approaches used on websites inspire you to learn more or to pay for a service?

After doing extensive research, ask yourself whether the message you are using to market your business is attracting clients. Is it making an impact? Dig deep and promote those unique aspects that potential clients would appreciate and need as a part of their healing process. Use creative words or images that support the point you are making. Instead of copying what someone else has done, focus your marketing on those features that distinguish you from others in the field. Maybe you have extensive experience and have worked in your field for more than 20 years — maybe your specialty is unique —you work with emotionally disturbed children or you assist cancer patients in attaining health and wholeness— maybe in addition to being an expert in your modality, you're also a medical intuitive; or maybe you've studied with someone famous whom everyone would know. The possibilities are endless. Tap into what makes you unique and creatively integrate that message into your marketing.

A great book that I read is *Made to Stick*, by Chip and Dan Heath. I mention this book because they address the question, "What makes ideas stick?" Why do we remember some ideas, products, services and stories and not others? This book makes you think about ways to effectively market and to teach so that your advertisements and words stick.

Exercise 10: Setting Your Message Apart - Assess your marketing materials and the language you use to convey your service. What is unique about your service or the way you perform it? What new and creative ways can you use to describe what you do that will make you stand out among the rest? What new and creative words or phrases can you use to speak about your business?

Starters – Get a good business card made. Consider making a menu card. Write articles to put on your website that explain your modality.

Growers – Evaluate your marketing and make any changes. Where can you submit articles outside of your website? Start a newsletter to send out to your email list. What unique ways can you get the word out to grow your business?

Expanders – Contact your local newspaper and get featured in an article. Read your marketing material. How can you use wording to set your message apart from others so that you stand out?

OTHER VALUABLE MARKETING IDEAS

Business Neighbors and Key Influential People

If your business is located in a business park or shopping center, make an effort to meet the other business owners. Tell them about your service(s) and give them a card or one of your brochures. Offer them the opportunity to receive a discounted or free session. Offer this discount to nearby doctors, dentists, or therapists who treat the type of client that you'd like to work with. If your business is near a school, introduce yourself to the wellness coordinator, the principal or health officer or to all three. Let them know that you can help their teachers and administrators to reduce stress and stay well. Offer them a discount. Teachers usually do receive discounts and they deserve them. Ask if you can provide flyers, brochures or discount coupons for the teachers' mailboxes.

Approach key people in your area who are influential and could provide referrals. Offer to do a discounted session on town council members or other influential people. They will spread the word about your service. Form or join a weekly breakfast business brainstorming group. As previously discussed, join Alignable.

Other Ideas

Take marketing workshops or classes offered by the Small Business Administration or SCORE or your local community college. Wearing a polo shirt with your company logo on it may elicit conversations with the public about your line of work. Join your local Chamber of Commerce. Teach a non-credit class at your local community college.

When I asked a friend of mine, an acupuncturist, who has a thriving and growing business, how she built her business, she said that word of mouth and referrals grew her practice. However, she noted that in March 2007, a client and friend published an article in a well-known local magazine about acupuncture and how it is effectively being used to get rid of wrinkles. In the article, the author discussed my friend's acupuncture business and added a picture of her that was used in the magazine as well. This is great exposure! Her business expanded substantially. Even though my friend did not ask her client to write the article, her client who had experienced the benefits of her service, thought it was worthwhile to let others know. Do you know someone that is a freelance writer? Can you get them to write an article about you?

Some practitioners working in spas and wellness centers must do their own marketing even though many big named spas do generate steady streams of clients. If you want the clients to request you for the service, then you need to market yourself. If you work in a spa or wellness center that is not as well known, then you must play a more active role in marketing your services. The spa or wellness center has the challenge to become known in the area where it is located. It has a budget for marketing in which it is marketing all of its products and services, not just yours.

When you work in a spa or wellness center, it is important that everyone working there be onboard to help that business to grow. The center's success is your success. Your success impacts the business as well. In order to grow your business at a center or spa, make sure that you are out in that community where the business is located. You want to be talking to the other businesses, local people, and the medical community letting them know who you are, where you work and what you offer as well as what the center offers.

In many cases, I have seen practitioners blaming the spa or center for their lack of success claiming that the center did not do enough marketing. With the minimal effort these practitioners were putting out to let the world know that they existed there, they would not be successful if they were out hosting their own business. To be successful, you need to participate in all the inner and outer aspects that create success even if you rent space or work for a spa or center.

You might want to find out what your spa or wellness center's vision and goals are and support and collaborate with holding that vision for the business. You made the choice to work there, either because you did not want to go out and take on the expense of renting a space on your own or you believed that this business would make getting clients easier. Whatever your reason for choosing this arrangement, commit yourself to looking at ways that you can market your services as well as the business and then follow through.

If you decide one day to venture out on your own, you will have mastered the marketing end of running your own business. That will be one thing that supports your success and one less thing you have to learn.

Your Sign

I am not talking about your astrology sign. When you visit a business or are looking for one as you navigate your way to it, what is the first think that you look for? A sign telling you which building the business is in. One very important aspect of launching a successful holistic health business is letting the world know that your business exists by having the right sign posted on site. Some holistic health businesses wait weeks or months trying to save up money or just plain save money instead of putting out a professional sign letting the world see that they exist. Many choose to put up a banner type signage in their front window made from computer paper or nylon/plastic sheets. How cheap does that look?

If you choose to rent space outside your home for your holistic health business, then financing for a professional commercial sign should be budgeted. Your sign or lack thereof is your face to the world. Do you want to make a welcoming impression or do you want to remain anonymous?

I once visited a place that was planning an open house. It was located in a complex of three buildings. Even though I had the address, the business was invisible to me. There were no signs at all, not even a cheap banner or plate on the door. I asked the owner about the sign and she said that she was waiting until the money started coming in before purchasing a sign. I attended the subsequent open house because I was scheduled to give a talk that day. The only people that were there were the speakers and a few of the owner's friends. Everyone commented about the lack of a business sign and how hard it was distinguishing which suite was hers, because there were so many empty suites. To them, her office looked like just another empty suite. How do you think it would appear to customers?

Many shopping centers and business plazas list their tenants on their sign that faces the main road. You most likely will not have much of a say about what that looks like, but you can inquire and work some terms into the lease before you sign. The signage over your unit, store front, business office is normally the holistic health owner's responsibility. Some commercial property management companies can take a month or more to get your business listed on their sign. It is very important that your own sign on your unit is up by the time you do your grand opening. Most companies will put this temporary sign in their window or over their doorway.

Most signs contain the company name and logo. The sign should give the consumer a good idea of what your business is about. The color and shapes of the letters should set a tone. It should be bright and big enough to let people know that you are here. If it is too small, people will need to strain to see it and they won't bother. It should also not be too extreme or it will turn off people who are looking to relax and find refuge in a peaceful atmosphere. The colors need to be seen from the road and also exude a sense of relaxation. The sign sets a tone for what a customer might expect to experience when entering your business. You shouldn't make your sign too busy or potential customers might be leery or turned off. Also, the "busier" the sign, the more expensive it will be.

A good sign draws people closer. It piques interest in what the company about. It feels friendly and makes people feel comfortable about going in to learn more.

When a new business comes into a commercial business area, the sign announces the business to the people visiting the other businesses and to those driving or walking by the area. Without a sign, your business is invisible or to put it bluntly – to customers your business does not exist. No matter how many affirmations you are saying each morning, no one will see you or walk in.

Bad signage or no sign tells your potential customers:

- You are not serious about your business
- You are temporary
- You are cheap
- You don't want people to find you

The effects of bad signage or no sign:

- Makes people question whether you are legitimate, or a fly-by-night business
- Makes the public question your professionalism
- Makes it hard for people to find your business
- Makes it hard for people to recognize that you exist – it makes you invisible
- Turns people off

Once you get people to come closer to learn more, make sure your hours of operation are on the door along with a phone number for customers to make appointments or ask questions. If you have a window on your office front, include an 8 ½ X 11 sheet of paper with your upcoming activities or a list of services that you provide. Include your Internet address, so that prospective clients can learn more about you and the services that you provide.

If you work from your home, having a sign can be tricky. It lets your neighbors know what you do. The blessing can be that you let your neighbors know that your services are available. It can also be a negative thing if you live in a very conservative area that is not open to holistic health. However, I continue to see things changing in the right direction. A lot of people that were once not very open to holistic services are now joining in. Most signage for home based businesses can be tastefully placed under the mailbox that is out on the road. It can also be placed on the house next to the front door or on a porch railing. Most home business signs are just big enough to let customers see where you are located and let those who walk by discover you and your services. Some communities and counties have their own rules about home businesses and about hanging signs, so find out what they are before you announce yourself to your community.

IT'S YOUR BUSINESS

In order to be successful, you need to treat everything that you are doing as a business. Many practitioners in the field of holistic health have told me they do not want to get caught up in the "old business paradigm" and "do that business stuff." Well, guess what? If your practice is your means of support, then it is a business and it is time to educate yourself and to get serious. In order for your practice/business to grow, you need to treat the business aspects of your business with the same seriousness and professionalism that you provide your services.

At first when I offered my services part-time and worked a full-time day job, I treated my service as providing opportunities to assist others at a discounted price. I wasn't focused on running a business, but instead I felt that my work was allowing me to do what I loved while learning more about energy dynamics and expanding my medical intuitive skills. I did save my receipts and paid taxes, but did not look into the write-offs that I could have taken. When I realized that this is what I wanted to do for a living, my energy, thoughts and actions changed. It became my business and I increased my prices. By that time, my clients understood the value of what they were getting and did not complain.

It's your business. So treat it seriously. Stop putting your receipts in an envelope for the end of the year. Get an accounting program. Find out what your options are and take action accordingly. Open a business checking account. Consult with an accountant. A reputable accountant can assist you with registering your company with the state, setting up your accounting program on your computer, calculating your tax liabilities, educating you regarding write offs, and choosing retirement investment options based on the business structure you have chosen. An accountant can provide a wealth of knowledge.

If you want to retain the revenue that you are generating, then make sure to keep and organize your receipts for all expenses. It's what you keep that counts! If the IRS decides to audit your books, you'll want to have all the supporting information to show that you are working in compliance with the law. So save your bank and credit card statements and pay your bills on time.

Want to run a successful and thriving holistic health business? Make sure you respond to texts, phone calls, and emails in a timely manner. Keep your website up to date and keep your place of business clean and orderly. Make sure your database of email contact information is up to date and have all those important contacts in your cellphone and have that information backed up into the cloud.

When starting your business, buy only those items that are necessary to create a nice and functional workspace. Make good buying decisions and put off the more expensive items until you are generating income. As you earn money, prioritize your spending so that you buy only what is needed to help you to expand your business.

Don't overlook the importance of dressing appropriately for a given situation. Are you networking? Then dress up. Are you doing a massage session? Dress neatly and comfortably. I have been to many workshops and received many holistic health sessions, and I do look at the appearance of the facilitator. Some people look like they just rolled out of bed and others were overdressed. On average, though, most practitioners and therapists were dressed appropriately for the service they were providing.

Creating Business Alliances

Your expertise in massage therapy, energy work, counseling, reflexology or yoga, etc. may be a good fit with other conventional and energetic healing businesses. Talk to other holistic health professionals and let them know about your services. You might be able to help each other by combining your modalities to assist clients in finding balance and in healing. For example, say you're a chiropractor or acupuncturist who is treating one aspect of a client's problem, but you notice that an emotional component needs to shift for the healing to be complete. Refer the client to another practitioner who can work with this piece, and with the client's permission provide background information to the other practitioner.

Within the purview of my Reiki and Medical Intuitive business, I work with doctors, nurse practitioners, naturopaths, chiropractors, and massage therapists in collaborating on client treatments (always with the client's written permission). Such collaboration can really speed up the healing process for a client. The old saying that two heads are better than one is very true. Just think about the possibilities of an acupuncturist working with a physician's patients, or a reflexologist working in a physical therapy practice. How about massage therapists receiving referrals from obstetricians? The possibilities are endless.

Also, if you are just starting out, you might want to consider sharing or renting office space with another practitioner or with a doctor or chiropractor who has an established practice and can refer clients to you.

In order to create business alliances with other health practitioners, you need to let them know what you do, and how their clients/patients can benefit from your service. Offer to take them to lunch to talk about your services or offer them an opportunity to attend your workshop or receive a session at a discount or for free. The more they understand what it is that you do and the benefits that you can provide, the more likely you will establish an alliance or get referrals. Consider offering "professional discounts" to other holistic health providers. They can be a great source for referrals.

In Home Office or Renting Space

Many therapists and practitioners ask whether it is better to set up shop in their home or in a rented space. For each person the benefits and reasons for doing so are different. Below are some issues you might want to consider in setting up your business in your home or in a rented facility.

If you are thinking about working in your home consider the following:

- Check any Homeowners' Association or condo restrictions.
- Are you and the other people in your home comfortable with having your clients come into your living space?
- Is there a bathroom easily accessible to where you will be holding your sessions or will clients need to walk through your home to get to the bathroom?
- Is your home handicapped accessible or does it need to be for your clients?
- Is your home located near potential clients and easy to find?
- Is adequate parking available for your clients? Especially if you are working with groups, is there enough parking for everyone?
- Is your room dedicated to your business or is it a multipurpose room, which might send mixed signals?
- Does the room you are using provide privacy?
- Does it have a door? Is your home quiet enough for your practice?
- Do you have small children who might be tempted to interrupt you?
- Do you have a separate entrance for your clients? This is not necessary, but is helpful.

If you are thinking about renting a space or sharing a space outside your home consider the following:

- How much is the rent?
- Will you still be able to make money after paying the rent?

- Is it possible to share this space with another practitioner or therapist?
- How much work needs to be done, and how much money will you need to spend in order to make this space useable for your practice? How long will this process take?
- Is the space large enough to do everything that you plan to do?
- How easy is it to travel to?
- Is it close to a main road?
- Is the space quiet and private?
- Is there a lot of competition nearby?
- Are there businesses nearby to advertise your services to?
- Are there businesses nearby that may detract from your business?
- What is the landlord liable for and what are you responsible for?
- How often can the rent be raised, and how easy or difficult is it to end the agreement?
- Can you grow your business in this location?

If you are sharing space with someone or renting from a wellness center or spa, you might want to consider the following:

- How much is the rent and how often will it be raised? Are you required to sign an agreement?
- Will the center book appointments for you?
- Does the center provide the furnishings for the room you are renting?
- Are you allowed to bring in and leave your personal items in your workspace?
- Do you feel emotionally and physically comfortable when you enter this business space?
- What vibes does the overall place emit?
- If you share the space with others, do they leave it neat and clean and do they emit positive energy?
- Do they leave the space ready for you to use after they have finished, or do you have to go in and tidy up before you can begin work?

- Is there space in the room for your working tools and personal items as well space for your clients to place their belongings?
- When working in this space, does it feel right to you?
- Does the location of this business have the potential to generate clients for you?
- Will other therapists or practitioners located in this space refer clients to you or are there already others offering the same service that you offer?

Your Professional Workspace

Your workspace is a very important part of your practice. It needs to be aesthetically pleasing to you and to your clients. It should be easy to travel to and easy to access. If there are a lot of steps, is there an elevator? The area should be clean, organized, and uncluttered. It should exude peace, comfort and serenity. Burning candles is fine, but be aware that some clients have allergies to candles or scents. If you expect to work with people with physical disabilities, make sure your workspace can accommodate them.

Your room should emit positive energy. Make sure your space feels like it is yours and is set up in a way that allows you to maneuver while working. When I first set up my workroom in our home, besides my table, everything else in the room was furniture left over from the move. It was a mix-and-match array of chairs, a daybed, and a dresser. I did not feel comfortable with the bright wall color. So after a couple months of feeling uncomfortable in the space, I got rid of furniture and did a total room makeover. My clients commented about the positive transformation. For me, the new room set up felt balanced and resonated calmness.

Your clients can tell on some level when the energy in the room is off. You need to clear away any toxic energy either at the end of the day, between clients (depending on the session) or at the end of the week. Burning sage, lighting a candle or using some other method with the intention to clear the energy, will make a great difference. If you have crystals in your workspace, make sure you take them out of the room at least quarterly and clear them before bringing them back into your workspace. Your attitude when you are working on others is also important. Make sure you are in a positive and healthy state. Otherwise, call your clients and reschedule.

Exercise 11: Your Professional Workspace - Go into your workspace and remove clutter or anything that does not belong there. Look around. Have you made this room yours? If you share a space with others, bring in some items that make you feel like the space is yours.

Overcoming Issues with Money and Competition

If you are really serious about making your holistic health practice your life's work, then you will need to visit your issues or fears around charging and collecting money for your services. Some people believe that holistic health providers should do their work for free or for reduced rates. They reason that since your ability to help others is a gift, you should offer it for free.

In fact, we pay many gifted people to fix our computers, to repair plumbing or electrical issues. We know up front that we are going to be charged for their talents. Your gift and training are no different. This idea that we should not charge for our particular gifts comes in part from the messages that we as practitioners have sent out to the universe. In the workshops that I have taught, I have heard practitioners say time and again, "How could I charge for this gift that I have been given?" We need to stop putting this thinking out into the universe and instead own the gifts that we are given, gifts that are here to financially support us! If you want to make money, you need to accept in your psyche that you deserve to make money. Money is just one more form of an energy exchange.

Another belief that keeps practitioners from attracting clients and money is that "It takes at least 2-3 years to build a sustaining business." Well if you believe this, then this will be your truth. Work on releasing negative and limiting beliefs. Free yourself up on the inner levels to attain your outer earning goals.

According to the National Institute of Health, over 49 percent of the US population pays to receive some type of holistic care, and that number continues to grow. With proper advertising, along with some leg work of your own to market your business, business will flow your way. If it is too scary for you to go solo with your practice, work for a holistic center, gym or spa to build a clientele before going out on your own.

Instead of viewing others in your field as competitors, remind yourself that there is enough work for everyone to be happily employed. When working with or talking to other practitioners, be happy for their successes. The alternative—feeling jealousy or envy about others' success—not only may direct negative energy to the other person, but can also create disharmony in your business and within yourself.

If you find yourself feeling anxious about money—feeling that you don't have enough or never will have enough—you may end up creating blocks in your life that will substantiate these beliefs. Work with affirmations and imagery to help move past the fear into an awareness that you will be provided for abundantly. You might try some of the following affirmations: "I am abundant." "My business is personally and financially successful." "My calendar is filled with paying clients." "My classes are filled with students." Imagine this as you say it, seeing and feeling it in your body.

Several successful therapists have shared their strategies with me: they post affirmations on the inside of their calendar/scheduling book, they also put a large sticker on the outside of their date book that reads "Abundance Book." When they pick up the calendar or look at it they are affirming their abundance.

Fees

At some point you transition from offering free services (when you are still learning) to charging a fee for your service. Call places nearby that offer the same services you do and ask what they charge. Make sure you do not over price or underprice your service. I find that some practitioners are *money phobic metaphysicians*, a term that I have coined for those in this field who have problems with accepting money for their services or undercharge/undervalue what they do. In both cases they use the following reasons: it is unacceptable to receive money for "this gift of healing" or "people should not have to pay for *this type* of service," or because of lack of self-esteem, "I am not good enough to charge full price." This way of thinking is a form of self-sabotage. If you undercharge, you can harm the holistic health arena as a whole because clients may expect others to charge less. If you undercharge, you might not be able to support yourself and may have to work two jobs or change career fields all together. In order to grow your business, you will need income to support yourself, to market your business and to pay for those services that support your expanding business. Your clients will not value what you do until you value what you do. Charge appropriately for your services. Make sure your fees reflect the experience and training that you have.

A good practitioner deserves to be rewarded for his or her efforts. **Money is a form of energy.** If what you collect is not equivalent to what you have given, then you short-change yourself energetically. Continually short-changing yourself may mean that you'll end up suffering from a very large energy imbalance.

One phenomenon that I have witnessed and other practitioners have shared, is that when you work for free, often clients don't value what they are given and are not always appreciative of the gift. They might even call and cancel at the last minute. When you are doing free sessions, you give the perception that you do not value what you do. When clients pay for a session, they tend to take your advice more seriously because they are paying for it. They see the value in what they pay for.

A well-known international instructor shared with me his learning regarding setting fees. He said that at first he charged about $40 per session and his sessions were good. He was instructed to charge more and was at first resistant, but then reluctantly raised his prices. He found that when he raised his prices, the quality of his sessions improved immensely. When he asked his guides about this phenomenon, they responded by saying that the energy that he could now give had shifted to equal the energy (money) that he was receiving for his work. He no longer questioned his guidance to change his prices. He now charges $140 an hour and is booked up to four months in advance. One thing is important to remember, though: if you decide to raise your fees, notify your clients of the increase at least a month in advance.

When your clients begin paying you more than what you charge, it is a sign that you should adjust your prices. Sometimes clients will come out and tell you that you are not charging enough. When you decide that it is time to increase your prices, make sure tell your clients about the increase 60 days prior to raising your prices. They should not be surprised by your price increase. If you realize that you are under charging by a lot and want to raise your prices, do it a little at a time. Spread it out over several months. You do not want to lose all of your clients that have gotten used to paying a lesser price. You want to step it up gradually so that they get used to paying more. If you are questioned about the price increase, you can tell them that your prices reflect the experience and training that you have and the expertise that you offer.

Some practitioners offer discounts for purchasing several sessions in advance, making the cost $20 - $30 less overall or $5 to $10 less per session. This may be a useful strategy because clients may feel that they are getting a bargain and you are getting the money in advance guaranteeing the work. The practitioners that used this method usually delineate a reasonable time period that the sessions must be used in. For example, three sessions purchased at one time need to be used over a three-month period.

Other practitioners may offer bundle services offering a discount if all of their services are purchased. Such as a facial, pedicure and a manicure. They may end up offering a $25 discount off the total. Or they might offer a Reiki session and a sound therapy session at a discounted fee. This way the consumer is likely to purchase more if they feel they are getting a good deal and you are receiving the opportunity to get paid for additional services. A win for all.

Bartering works only when you have time to participate and if it benefits both providers. If you need the money, do not barter, unless it is really a service that you need as a part of your life.

If you are teaching workshops, make sure you are charging the going rate for the class (that is, if there are any other classes like it). If you undercharge, thinking that you will attract more students because you are less expensive, you are really hurting teachers overall in that modality. You are also hurting yourself in the future because people will expect your rates to be consistently cheaper across the board. You may also be undervaluing yourself. If you could afford to pay to take the classes, couldn't others? Do you want to attract students because you are inexpensive or because you are good? When you charge the going rate, you may see a difference in the kind of students that you attract. Value what you do, and others will value what you have to give.

When teaching workshops, it's a good idea to collect the full amount in advance for the class. This way you know how many people are really serious about signing up for your course. When students have paid in advance, they are more likely to show up for the class. I find that collecting the money the day of the class is too cumbersome and you need to make it easy on yourself. Teaching is a big enough responsibility for one day.

Exercise 12: Determining Your Fee - Call around and find out what other practitioners in your field are charging. Modify your fee if necessary.

Credit Card Options

Make it easy for your customers to pay you. Most people that I talk to do not carry cash or checks on them anymore. Every holistic health business needs to offer a credit card payment option. There are so many companies now that make it easy for you to take credit card payments. Paypal, Square, and Shopify all offer devices that you connect into your cell phone and tablets to receive payment. The money shows up into your bank account a day later, minus the company's fee.

Gift Certificates

Make sure you have gift certificates for sessions and classes available. Tell your clients about the gift certificates and consider posting a small sign in your work space stating, "Gift Certificates Are Available." Satisfied clients often want to share with a friend or family member the same valuable experience that they have received. You might also let your local realtor know that you offer gift certificates. Many realtors give certificates to their new homeowners as a thank you gift for doing business with them. Other professionals might want to do the same, so let folks know that you have certificates available and let people know that they make great thank you, congratulations, "I'm sorry," anniversary, and birthday gifts. Make sure that you have put an expiration date on each one.

Exercise 13: Creating a Gift Certificate - Make a gift certificate. Place a small sign in your treatment room that lets your clients know about the certificates. Make sure you indicate that you have gift certificates in your newsletter.

Creating a Niche

Look to expand the work that you do by learning skills that will benefit a particular group of people. One massage therapist that I know took a workshop on massage techniques to benefit golfers. She now advertises at three local golf courses. Find ways to make your practice unique in a way that might attract a particular type of client. You don't want to narrow your focus too much or you could end up limiting your business.

There are so many areas to specialize in. What do you feel passionate about when it comes to helping your clients? What additional training can you receive to become a specialist? One massage therapist that I know purchased a device that gets the lymph system moving. She felt like her clientele, which were mostly those 60 and above, could benefit from this service. She received training on how to use it and her appointments are all filled. Another massage therapist that I know decided to become a certified Ayurveda consultant. She now offers mind and body life-style consultations to help her clients stay healthy.

Another way to generate additional income is to sell a product or products that complement your modality and benefit your clients. If you decide to sell products, check into getting a sales tax identification number from your state, because some states require them and you will have to pay quarterly sales tax to your state.

Insurance

When you start receiving money for practicing your modality, make sure you have liability insurance. It protects you and your family's assets. The International Massage Association Hands on Insurance, and Namaste provide insurance for massage practitioners and energy workers and cover a wide variety of modalities. The International Association of Reiki Practitioners (IARP) provides insurance for Reiki practitioners. Some of these associations provide your name in their directories online so that you can receive referrals from people surfing the Internet and visiting their webpages. The insurance is affordable, and in the long run, could save you a lot of heartache and expense. The websites for these organizations are listed below:

www.internationalmassage.com,
www.handsoninusrance.com,
www.namasta.com/services/memberservices.php
www.iarp.org

Exercise 14: Exploring Insurance Options - If you do not already have insurance, look into getting it.

Freebies

Although working for free is not your goal, offering free services sometimes provides an opportunity for you to connect with potential clients or to gain referrals. When you decide to volunteer at a health fair or open house, make sure it is no more than a half-hour or an hour drive from your office. You want to make sure that you are investing your time and energy in something that that has a good possibility of bringing in clients. If you are working a health fair over two hours away, it is very unlikely that you will find clients who are willing to travel that far to receive a treatment. There are probably other massage therapists or healing arts therapists between your office and their home. When you work an event for free, choose wisely.

You might want to consider offering a professional discount or a free session to those who would be influential enough to generate referrals for you. If you do any form of holistic energy work, you might want to consider having an open healing share on a regular basis. Such a "share" offers an opportunity for practitioners to get together in order to practice on each other and you could open the share up to the public. You might want to begin the share by reviewing, for those who are unfamiliar, what they can expect, and how they can find out more information about Reiki. Make sure that you have informative handouts and flyers for your workshops and services available at these shares. This is an excellent way to generate interest in your holistic healing field as well as to educate the general public. If you need to rent space to hold the share, it's common practice to request a nominal charge of $5 to $15 for the session.

Consider offering free services at senior recreation centers, nursing homes, and churches. It's an excellent way to open up and truly share. The appreciation you will receive is wonderful. For me, it is an excellent opportunity to give back for all that the universe has given to me. We all are moved to provide a complementary session now and again, but it's important to find a healthy balance in how much free work we decide to do.

Seeking Professional Advice

Starting up or expanding a business can require you to file various documents with state and federal agencies as well as make monthly or quarterly tax payments. Many good accountants or small financial businesses specialize in helping people start or run their businesses and it is worth the money to seek their help. Your accountant can tell you exactly what forms need to be filled out in order to become incorporated. He or she can do that paperwork, but you can also do it yourself. Go to your state website to look for information on your state's laws regarding the type of business you are opening, as well as the laws around the business structure you are choosing.

When I realized that I would need to use software for accounting, I had to admit that I knew nothing about how to run the programs. My accountant came over to my home, loaded Quickbooks, and set up the accounts. He saved me a lot of time and headache. He also showed me how to reconcile my accounts monthly and walked me through the required quarterly state and federal tax filing. Without his help and advice, I would have been really lost in the world of electronic accounting and taxes. He also gave valuable advice on setting up a retirement account and on tips for understanding what can be deducted. You can also find many wonderful books on how to take tax deductions for those of us who are self-employed. Make sure you read at least one or two books on the subject.

Depending on your area of expertise, you might need to consult a lawyer, interior designer, a computer specialist, etc. Spending the money is usually worth it in the end. Any consultant that you pay is an expense that you can write off at tax time.

Other professionals that you might consider consulting are insurance brokers, computer website designers, computer repair technicians, marketing consultants, etc. It is a good idea to have a list of reputable support people set up ahead of time. Consult with other holistic health practitioners. Ask them about whom they would choose to provide such services. Word of mouth is your best tool for finding those who excel in their fields.

As I mentioned earlier, SCORE provides professional business advice. SCORE members are retired business professionals who offer expertise in a myriad of fields. They offer outstanding workshops at low cost, as well as one-on-one counseling for small businesses. Their goal is to help you to be successful and to provide advice and guidance, but in the final analysis, you are the one who has to do the work.

The Small Business Administration was created in 1953 as an independent agency of the federal government to aid, counsel, assist and protect the interests of small business concerns, to preserve free competitive enterprise and to maintain and strengthen the overall economy. The SBA helps Americans start, build and grow businesses. Through an extensive network of field offices and partnerships with public and private organizations, SBA delivers its services to people throughout the United States, Puerto Rico, the U.S. Virgin Islands and Guam. The SBA offers workshops, counseling, and mentoring services. Many of their resources are online, and they also have a chat room. They focus on helping all small businesses, with special emphasis on women, Native American and veteran-owned businesses. You can acquire a wealth of information and knowledge from this organization.

Keeping Good Records

If you are a social worker, nurse, acupuncturist, or massage therapist, you most likely are legally required to have some type of written record of your client sessions. No matter what modality you practice, anything that you write down about your clients must be kept in a locked file cabinet to ensure privacy. Of course, there is more to recordkeeping than simply maintaining privacy, so be sure that you know the legal requirements of your modality and follow them.

Make sure that you get the name, address, telephone number, and email address of each client. If you work for a wellness center or other place of business that maintains client files, make sure you keep your own records, as well. Many practitioners start out working for someone else in order to build a steady clientele before they move out on their own. It's important to keep good client records so that you can inform clients when you are ready to start your own business. You will probably send out emails or postcards letting clients know how and where they can find you. You can even offer them a discount for their first visit to your new place. After you are up and running, host an open house in which you serve light snacks.

Client contact information is very important because it gives you a means by which to provide reminders to clients to schedule their next appointment, buy a gift certificate for a friend, or attend your next class. Make sure you collect this essential information for each client.

Keep good records of your expenses. This will determine the amount of taxes you will have to pay. It is worth taking the time to establish good record keeping habits. This will save you time and money.

Learn to Manage Your Time

When you learn to work smarter, you find better ways to manage your time. As a business owner, time management is very important. Here are some tips for better time management.

Stop overscheduling yourself. Many practitioners will take a client even though they have taken their maximum number for the day. They are thinking clients are money; instead of thinking "What other day can I schedule this client?" Continual overbooking or scheduling too many things in one day creates burnout. You can't work very well if you are burned out.

Prioritize. What important business related activities can you complete before your first client? Most people have more energy in the morning. Get your goals completed while you are fresh. When you put chores off to later, sometimes they do not get done.

Eliminate those chores that do not add value to your business. Get rid of the busyness that is not growing or expanding your business.

Return phone calls, texts, and emails at a set time during your day, unless it is something that really needs your immediate attention.

Stop spending so much time looking at social media, reading emails, or playing games on your phone. These are time wasters. Set a certain amount of time a day at a designated time each day to do these things. You will find that you begin to lose interest in them and get more business accomplished.

Get organized. The more organized you are, the more time you will save and you will experience less frustration because of being disorganized. If this is a challenge for you, hire someone to organize you.

Always be on time for your clients. Be ready for them before they get there. If you are late and not ready, you will lose clients.

Engage in a healthy lifestyle. Numerous studies have shown that people who eat right, exercise and engage in healthy choices, are more productive. It inspires confidence that you are going to be able to help your clients reach their goals if you look healthy yourself. It serves you personally and in your business.

Have unscheduled time. This allows you to free up your mind, to relax, and recharge. This also makes you more productive during scheduled work times.

Create alone time in the silence. This helps you to find peace, reconnect with your passion, and will reduce stress. When you are less stressed, your joy for what you are doing shows. You radiate and attract more business.

SPREADING YOUR WINGS

You have now prepared to market yourself by delivering your talk to groups that might want or require your service. Before you take your one-hour talk out into the world, reflect on why you are giving such a talk. Is it to gain clients or students, educate potential consumers about your modality, or fill your classes, or is it because you are looking for something to do?

When you reach a point at which you have a full and thriving business, and can no longer expand your business, you might want to forgo the free talk as well as paid advertisements and let referrals keep your business growing and filled. Let's hope that you get that successful! For now, make sure you are looking to present your talk to audiences and groups that are open to hear what you have to share; otherwise, you could be wasting your time.

When you contact the organizations about offering your talk, speak in a professional manner. Be ready to be given several names and numbers before reaching the right person. You might be asked to provide a cover letter, a resume, and an outline of your proposed talk or you could be offered an opportunity to speak as a result of the phone conversation.

Places to Consider Giving Your Talk

Hospitals or medical centers—Is your audience the professional staff, such as doctors, nurses, social workers or therapists, or is it the public that uses that facility? Determining the audience will help you figure out whom to contact in the hospital—either the person in charge of hospital training (training of their employees) or someone in the hospital's outreach, public relations, community relations, or wellness department. If you know someone who works there, ask them who they might suggest as your first contact.

Churches—Some churches are open to the holistic health arena. They might let you set up a healing and prayer group or let you demonstrate or talk about your specialty to members.

Businesses—Some big businesses have medical facilities and Wellness Programs and are interested in promoting activities that reduce stress. Be prepared to make lots of calls to get to the right person.

Health Fairs—If you rent a space or table at a health fair, you may have an opportunity to present a talk. These opportunities book up fast, so be sure to inquire before you reserve a space for the fair.

Communities of 55-Plus—These communities frequently have wellness or recreation facilities and managed activities and they often have a men's and a women's group. Baby Boomers are often keenly interested in maintaining good health and might be very receptive to your talk. You could generate a lot of new clients from this population and if you generate enough interest, you might even be able to set up a practice on site one or two days a week.

Newspapers—Scan your local newspaper for groups that are sponsoring speakers. These are usually listed under the headings "Community News" or "Community Activities," "Health Notes," "Religious Activities," or "Support Groups," etc. Contact names and numbers are usually provided. Check out the listing of groups and contact ones that would be open to hearing your talk and that would generate clients or students. You may never look at a newspaper the same way again! Articles can also be good leads for opportunities to present your talk or improve your business.

Women's Groups/Men's Groups—These are excellent places to present your talk and to generate new clients and referrals.

Professional Associations—Most professional organizations hold yearly conventions that sponsor various speakers or rent booth space to vendors. Take advantage of these opportunities.

Universities/Community Colleges—Find instructors and department heads who might be interested in integrating your talk into their curriculum, particularly in the fields of Allied Health. Some nursing schools dedicate a day out of the school year to introduce the students and faculty to a broader range of topics. Occupational therapy, physical therapy, nursing, massage, psychology, etc. are all departments that might benefit from your talk.

Local School System—If your field focuses on children, contact the principal or school board and offer to do some presentations to the PTA, the teachers or administrators.

YMCA/YWCA—These organizations usually offer workshops, which can be a good way to connect with your local community and get the word out about your specialty.

Local Health Food or Health Product Store—These stores promote good health. It only makes sense that they would love to have you come demonstrate your skill or provide a presentation. It helps if you can promote some of the store's products during your presentation. Contact the store manager or public relations person.

Local Health Club—Is there a racquetball club, a gym, or a Curves™ for women near you? Maybe you can offer your services there or offer to present your talk or leave some business cards or flyers.

Local Chamber of Commerce—Join your local Chamber of Commerce and talk to the group about the benefits of your service. Through networking, you may find that other members want you to speak to their own organizations about your service. See the Appendix for additional benefits received by joining your Chamber of Commerce.

It's unlikely that you will be paid for these talks, but the value lies in the opportunities you will have created to make an impression on a group of people with whom you would not normally have contact with. Providing talks can be very rewarding. Even if a specific talk doesn't result in clients or students, rest assured that you've taken a step in educating others on the benefits of your modality.

Medical professionals or business professionals can be great resources for suggesting new venues at which you can give your talk. You might be surprised at the great recommendations you receive and at how well these professionals are plugged in to local networks. They can get you the right person to contact or even get you an opportunity to speak for their own organization. A lot of times it is not what you know, but who you know that counts.

Be sure to dress professionally when giving your talk. Rehearse what you have to say for friends and family before you present it to the public. Your talk will make an impression. Make sure it is a good presentation that will generate interest among listeners and generate a desire for your service. If it goes well, consider asking the sponsor of your talk to put you on the schedule for a future speaking date.

Another option, for marketing yourself and becoming known to your community and the network of other practitioners, is to organize a holistic health fair. If you do not have the physical space to host one, you can contact your local community college Allied Health coordinator to cosponsor the event so that it can be held at the college. You can then invite other local holistic health practitioners to rent space and to give talks. It is a great way to connect with your immediate community and with potential clients. Make sure you start planning ahead of time and market the fare well in advance, so that it is very well attended.

There is a term out called evergreen. Like the evergreen trees that seem to be around forever, the content that you create for you talks should be reusable for other forums. Video parts of your talk and put that content on your website or on social media, or put the whole talk up on YouTube. Use the information for articles or for your blog. Think of all the different ways that you can reuse this valuable information. Maybe you can write a book or develop a class with it.

Credentials

In this complicated world of alphabet certifications and licensing, many organizations that invite you as a speaker will want a copy of credentials. Often, those reviewing your credentials may not regard certification as a Reiki Master, massage therapist, or certified Healing Touch practitioner as adequate because it isn't equivalent to holding a degree in fields such as nursing, social work and chiropractics. What I tell my students is to emphasize the highest training that they have had or a job title or position that they hold that adds to their credentials. One Reiki Master, who did not have a degree, was the head of his company's public relations department. When he used that title along with his Reiki Master certification, it seemed to open many doors in the holistic health arena. If you do not have a title or degree, you might want to consider furthering your education, if you believe that is necessary. It's your call and the decision likely depends on the doors that you want to open in the future. Many holistic healers are so good at what they do that their reputation opens doors for them, whereas others would benefit from a little more education to gain more skills in writing, communicating and operating a business.

If you do have certifications, you might want to tastefully display them in your treatment room. Resist the temptation to exhibit every certificate you ever received—you don't want to overdo it.

Spa Parties

One way to generate business and clients is to host a spa party. You can also have friends host your spa party or have a business sponsor one to benefit their employees. A spa party allows a group of four to eight people to pay a discounted fee in order to receive one of the services you offer and the services of other practitioners offering different modalities. Sometimes two or more practitioners may work together and more people can then participate. The host usually provides some snacks and drinks. The practitioners may give a short talk about their services to the group. The practitioners get paid to provide a sample (about a half hour massage or session) and they generate new clients or referrals. It's a win-win situation. The clients get a sample of services at a discount, and you get exposure to new clients.

Growers – Reach out to different groups and offer to give talks.

Expanders – Put together a mini conference or spa day including other therapists. Get the media to spread the word.

NETWORKING

Networking is key to your success. Make every outing an opportunity to network and generate business. Talk about what you do with everyone. If they seem turned off, respect where they are and stop talking. If you generate interest, give them a business card and refer them to your website.

When I went to a showing of an indie movie at a local bookstore, I knew the people that would be attending were my potential clients. I went early to network. During that time, I generated two Reiki students for a class, an opportunity to teach a crystal class at the location where the film was being screened, and another speaking engagement from someone I met at the movie. That speaking engagement, which I gave a month after the movie, generated eight new clients and five referrals from those clients.

Formal networking groups are easy to join. Whether you are in formal or informal networking situations, you're there to generate referrals, so speak up and be heard. Don't be a wallflower.

Networking

Join local networking groups. Some groups include members that represent various career paths and modalities. They meet weekly or monthly to share tips on how to generate success and they send referrals to other members. Other networking groups are bigger and provide opportunities for their members to present on topics related to their expertise. They usually invite the public in order to grow their network. Networks are great if you have the time to attend.

Here is some advice on networking from Dr. Robert Muller, Assistant Secretary-General for Economic and Social Services for the United Nations:

Decide to Network

Use every letter you write
Every conversation you have
Every meeting you attend
To express your fundamental beliefs and dreams
Affirm to others the vision of the world you want
Network through thought
Network through action
Network through love
Network through the spirit
You are the center of a network
You are the center of the world
You are a free, immensely powerful source
Of life and goodness
Affirm it
Spread it
Radiate it
Think day and night about it
And you will see a miracle happen:
The greatness of your own life.
In a world of big powers, media, and monopolies
But of four and a half billion individuals
Networking is the new freedom
The new democracy
A new form of happiness.

Networking groups can provide you with new ideas on marketing your service, problem solving information, and business opportunities. They sometimes involve sharing a meal. Some networking groups charge a fee while others are free. You can always start one of your own! Join your local Chamber of Commerce. It is usually inexpensive and there are many opportunities to network and meet people in different career fields who might benefit your business. If you plan to join a network group that charges membership fees, see if you can attend a few sessions for free or at a discount to assess whether the group is serious about giving referrals or if it just a night out to socialize with the guys/gals.

Many people do not feel comfortable going into groups where they may not know anyone. They say it makes them feel awkward and out of place. When you are self-employed this is one hurdle you need to get over. Even though I am an extrovert, these situations made me a little uncomfortable at first. I found that once I put myself out there, I met some amazing people, learned some information that was valuable and made some good connections. Here are some tips at making your networking experience more effective.

- Go to the meetings on a regular basis. When people see you at all the meetings, you look familiar to them and they begin to build trust and become interested in what you do. They will feel comfortable speaking with you.
- If networking events feel like a chore, pick the events that have speakers that you would enjoy or go to the outings that are fun. Some networking events are in restaurants, bars, or at a grand opening celebrations. When it is fun, you will enjoy going out and meeting new people. You can also host an event for your networking group in your healing studio. Maybe offer them a free sample of what you do with a short informational talk followed by questions and snacks.
- Seek out people that could be great potential clients and and/or can potentially give you lots of referrals. Maybe it is someone who has been very stressed and could use Reiki, a massage, or hypnotherapy. It could be someone who is talking about going to have surgery or is recovering from a physical issue. I would seek to connect with chiropractors, counselors, and psychologists. They seemed to be open and understanding of my work and world, and provided many of my referrals. They also became clients. If you meet someone at the meetings that could be a great referral provider, you might

want to offer them a free session. Get their contact information. If they are open to a session, follow up in a few days and give them dates and times when you are available. Make it happen.

- After you meet people at the meetings and get their business cards, connect with them on social media. This is another way to stay in touch and for your posts to inform them of what you are all about. They will get to know you better and may feel more comfortable with you.

- Lastly, when you go to networking meetings and events, don't sound desperate or too sales pitchy. Be genuine. The goal is to establish trust and relationships that will generate clients, referrals, and speaking opportunities.

When you think of networking, remember that you can do this at PTA meetings, community meetings, your golf or bicycle group outings, and your book clubs. You can talk about your successes or what you love about what you do. You do not want to be annoying, but you want your friends to understand the benefits of what you have to offer. What groups are you involved in? How can you let others know what you are doing?

If your spouse or significant other is comfortable with the idea, he or she can network for you and hand out your cards. Oftentimes our loved ones are our biggest supporters, so make sure they have your updated information to give to others. But do not be disappointed if they are not into networking for you. I only recommend this if they are comfortable with doing so.

Business Network International (BNI) is a worldwide organization with networking groups somewhere in your area. They usually meet at times that are convenient for most members, either before work or at lunch. BNI is a business and professional networking organization that offers members the opportunity to share ideas, contacts and most importantly, referrals. I specifically mention this group because it has been around for over 20 years and has a good reputation. Each chapter only takes one person per professional specialty, so you won't be competing with others in the chapter for referrals. Their goal is to generate referrals for members. You can find them on the web at www.bni.com. Advice given to me from practitioners that have investigated BNI groups is to visit a few chapters to find one that you feel comfortable joining.

Benefits of BNI Membership

In addition to periodic workshops on networking, BNI offers:

- Substantially increased referrals
- Tools to network more effectively, including an orientation giving the "Formula for Success" in BNI, a badge, a vinyl card holder to carry members' business cards, referral slips, and marketing materials.
- Participation in up to 52 networking meetings per year.
- Quarterly newsletters with educational material on networking, public speaking, and business.
- Participation in business trade shows (where you'll have an opportunity to market your chapter and your business).

Referrals

Referrals are a sure way to create success. Think outside the box about who could be a potential source of referrals besides family and friends. How about your family physician, dentist, chiropractor, therapist, mechanic, lawyer, investment broker, handyman, minister, etc.? I receive referrals from my chiropractor, two psychologist friends, a counselor, a lawyer, a doctor, several nurses, an acupuncturist, an insurance agent, my investment broker, government contractors, accountants, and a nutritionist. Because I receive referrals, I always make sure to return the favor and give clients business cards when they voice a need for a particular service.

One statement that you can use in soliciting referrals is, "I am expanding my business and am ready to take on new clients." This sounds much better than simply asking, "Can you send me some referrals?" Make sure you always carry business cards and keep a ready supply in your treatment room for clients. If you are looking for referrals, make sure you give each person several cards and that you take the time to thank the person who sent you the referral.

Health insurance companies now have networks of complementary care or holistic care providers. In order to be included in this network of providers, contact them. They will ask for references and require that you provide your service to their members at a discount that they have predetermined. Another angle to investigate to increase clientele is to find out which health insurance providers offer Flex Spending Accounts. Some holistic services are now being approved for flex spending dollars; these services include: massage, chiropractics, and acupuncture. Get on the list to become an approved provider.

Present your clients with opportunities to provide you referrals, while also benefiting them. One way is to reward them with a $10 or $20 coupon toward one of your services when they provide you a referral.

Another great way to generate new clients and to receive referrals is to join your local Chamber of Commerce. By joining your Chamber of Commerce, you can enjoy many benefits yourself and meet others who might be interested in your service. One massage therapist told me that after he joined his town's Chamber of Commerce, many members called and made appointments. In turn, they referred to him many of their business associates. His business is booming.

Ask the universe for referrals. You do not need to be in charge of how your clients find you. Be open—very open! Tell your guides and angels to send you clients and/or students. Sometimes clients have found me in the most interesting ways. One person literally ran into me when I worked for the federal government. She said that her guidance was to go out into the hallway and that Dawn would be out there. She was not sure which office I worked in so she began walking the hallways. Within two minutes our paths crossed, and she said, "You are just the person I was looking for." Another encounter was in an elevator. I was balancing on one foot while tying my shoe, as the elevator was moving. My balancing act impressed a part-time karate instructor so much that we began talking and he expressed an interest in my services. Clients and students can come from anywhere, so be open.

Starters - Your networking begins by talking to almost everyone that you meet when you are out in public. When you are standing in line, talk to the person behind you. When you are in the dentist's office, talk to the dentist and the assistants. You get it, start talking. Give out your cards, and collect emails.

Growers and Expanders - Attend some networking groups to see which ones resonate with you. Take your business and menu cards. Offer to be a speaker at one of the meetings.

Expanders - Host a networking event at your location. Become seen as a leader in your community.

BECOME A CONTINUING EDUCATION PROVIDER

Your state or national career boards may require professionals in some career fields to continue their education by taking classes that provide continuing education units or contact hours. Different boards refer to these teaching units as continuing education units, contact hours, or continuing education credits. The time calculated to determine what equals one unit also differs among the boards.

If you are a teacher, becoming a provider of these Continuing Education Credits (CEs) or contact hours can attract students to you from these fields. Before applying to teach in such a program, make sure that what you teach is relevant to the fields in which you are seeking to provide CEs or contact hours. Talk to your friends and family employed in the fields of social work, counseling, nursing, physical and occupational therapy, massage, acupuncture, etc. Find out if they have a requirement to get continuing education. You can call your state department of health office and find out if these fields have continuing education requirements. Be sure to inquire about whether it is a state or national requirement.

If the state has a requirement for continuing education, find out if you can become a CE provider through the relevant state board for that career field; otherwise, you might need to check with a regional or national organization that approves CE providers. Then go online and find that organization. They will usually have their provider application information online. If not, you can ask them to mail you the package of information to become a CE provider.

My experience is that if you choose this path, you are in for a lot of work up front. In a lot of cases forms can now be filled out online. There are some fees for having your applications reviewed. In most cases, I have found that it is worth the work. Some boards have a one-time fee for all the classes submitted, while others charge a fee for each class. Most fields have a requirement that you renew (by going through the same process) every two or three years.

Most career fields that you apply to will review your credentials. Some require a Bachelor's degree as a minimum to be teaching their professionals. The first time I received an application for CE provider it sat on my desk for six months. I was overwhelmed by the paperwork. But when I dedicated a couple of days to the process, I found that I was able to complete it quickly. Most applications can be filled out online now. A lot different than when I started in the 1990s.

At a minimum, CE and contact hour applications require that you submit the following: an application form; an outline for each course with timetables for each session of your workshop; copies of your advertising brochures or flyers; a bio; plus copies of your own certificates showing you can teach the subject matter; certificates that you intend to hand out to students; and an evaluation that you will distribute to students.

Most boards require that you maintain a database of the students attending your classes for up to five years. The database must include the student's name and address, the date of the class, and the number of CEs the student received. The approval process can take from one to three months to be completed after you submit it to the appropriate board. Be prepared for requests for more information, corrections, revisions or even offers to advise you in navigating the application process (for a fee).

After you submit your package, within two months you will be informed of either acceptance or denial. After you have completed the application process and are approved, it is time to find the correct avenue to advertise your classes. Each field will usually have a state or national newsletter. Find the state newsletter or website and place your advertisement. You want to make all this work worthwhile. Find out if you can write an article relating the benefits of your workshop to that career field for the newsletter. For more information on becoming a CE provider, check out my online course on how to become a CE provider at

http://energy-transformations.teachable.com/

MANAGING YOUR GROWING BUSINESS

At some point your business will begin to take off. Naturally, this will be a very exciting time, but it also means that you may need to find new ways to manage your time and your clients, do paperwork, file taxes, and keep appointments. You may also find it challenging to find ways to transition back to your own life after a busy workday.

One fundamental asset to managing your growing business is to get organized and stay organized. When you fall behind in returning text and phone calls, answering emails, paying business-related bills or entering your receipts into the proper accounts, it can cause you to lose ground. An inability to manage the practicalities of a business can be a stumbling block to success. So start off on the right foot by creating good habits from the outset. Make sure you know how much money is in your accounts. Return texts, calls and emails promptly. Manage how much time you spend on social media everyday so that it does not take away your valuable time.

Choose a specific time each day to deal with correspondence, then you won't be interrupted periodically throughout your workday. Limit your business-related calls to five minutes or less, unless there is a real need to go longer. Otherwise, your clients will think you have all day just to chat with them. Do the same with your marketing and accounting tasks: limit those tasks to a single day during the week, so that you don't end up becoming overwhelmed by these tasks and falling behind. The more grounded and organized you are, the better off you and your business will be.

When you created your original vision statement, you probably had a clear idea of how many clients you wanted to have per week or per month. As I approached my goal of 20 clients a week plus fully enrolled classes (I was teaching at least two workshops a month, usually more),

I began to feel like I was losing energy. I didn't have a moment to myself. I was becoming increasingly anxious as I tried to find time to prepare for my workshops and do everyday tasks, such as cooking dinner. So I had to revise my original vision. I learned that I just couldn't manage 20 clients a week. So for my best interest, I revised my Vision Declaration and did the inner work to create a new dynamic. I also stopped taking clients on weekends.

If you are having problems managing your business, take some time to identify what the issues are and look into addressing them in order to find a solution quickly.

Tips for Letting Your Clients Know They Are Important

The more you can honor and respect your clients, the more repeat business and referrals you'll have. There are many ways to let your clients know that they are important. Here are some suggestions:

- Once your clients arrive, greet them with a smile
- Keep your cell phone turned off.
- Create a safe and comforting space for clients to receive deep work.
- Be respectful of your clients' time and yours. Book your sessions so that you are not consistently late.
- Honor your clients' time. Don't exceed the allotted time unless you have their permission.
- Be present. Avoid distractions and really listen to what clients are telling you.
- Maintain eye contact. This shows you are listening and are present.
- Consider keeping notes on each session. (This is a legal requirement for some holistic health careers.) Review your notes before the next session. When clients arrive, ask about any issues from their prior visit, and whether things have

improved. Clients will be impressed that you remember details about the session and that you want to follow-up.

- Cancel appointments if you are ill or if clients are ill.
- Answer your emails and return phone calls quickly.
- When appropriate, follow up with your clients, especially if they have had surgery or are going through a difficult time.
- Send a thank you note for a referral.
- Gratitude.

Exercise 15: Let Clients Know They Are Important - Make a list of actions you can take to ensure that your clients feel important. Begin putting them into practice. Be sincere.

ETHICS

Ethics can be defined as standards of conduct, moral judgments, or a system or code of morals of a particular person, group or profession. Making sure that you conduct yourself in an ethical manner is an integral part of your business. In order to maintain or create a healthy successful holistic business, you must be ethical in all aspects of assisting your clients and in your business dealings as well.

Here are some ethical considerations for holistic health practitioners and educators to keep in mind:

- Be honest about your certifications and qualifications. Have those certificates available for your clients or students to see if requested.
- Educate your clients so that they understand the service that you provide and what they can expect from your modality.
- Be sincere in your commitment to provide the highest quality of care.
- Use good judgment and appropriate touch at all times.
- Always maintain the confidentiality of what you discuss with your clients.
- Always maintain a clean and orderly workspace.
- When you encounter your clients in public, do not discuss the details of their treatment (this is not good for either of you).
- Remember to practice good hygiene. Clients will be turned off by body odors or cooking odors, such as garlic or onion. Avoid wearing fragrance or perfume because many people have allergies even to the most mild of fragrances.
- Provide treatment only if you feel that your modality will be good for the client.
- Empower your clients and students to be active in their healing process.

- Never diagnose or prescribe and never recommend that a client change a prescribed treatment. You can share your impressions, but you can't diagnose unless you are a doctor.
- Encourage clients to seek professional conventional medical advice when you suspect that it would be useful.
- Respect your clients' and students' views and religious/spiritual paths.
- Respect your clients' right to end treatment or to seek another form of treatment.
- Respect other disciplines and other practitioners and refrain from criticizing others. Encourage clients to seek information about the choices that they make.
- Be respectful and sensitive about boundary issues and needs of clients and students.
- Do not touch the breast or genital areas. During energy work, the client should remain clothed. During massage, a sheet should cover the areas of a client's body that aren't being worked on.
- If clients need to undress in order to receive services, make sure they have a private space to do so.
- If you are teaching, be on time and end your classes on time. Do not allow students to dictate the flow of the class. Present your information logically and avoid an appearance of being scattered or interrupted. If students feel confused, they may not return for future classes.
- Do not apply pressure to clients or students to take classes. Encourage them to follow their own hearts' calling as to when they're ready to move forward. On the other hand, make sure that you feel that they are ready to advance before teaching them the higher levels of holistic health training.
- Never abuse your authority or power. Remain mindful of your ego.
- Be actively working on your own healing.
- Support the holistic health community by promoting high standards of practice.

- Conduct all business in a professional manner with honesty and integrity.
- Do not engage with your clients in any sexual conduct or activities.
- Respect your students' right to seek other teachers.
- Seek excellence by regularly assessing your strengths, limitations and effectiveness and by attending continuing education opportunities and training.
- Avail yourself of other practitioners. Learn what they do.
- Practice what you preach!

Exercise: 16: Discerning Your Ethical Strengths and Weaknesses - Review the suggestions above and then list your strengths and weaknesses.

Exercise 17: Discerning Your Ethics - List two or more ethical standards that relate to your field of holistic health.

HEALTHY BOUNDARIES

Creating healthy boundaries for yourself and your business is extremely important. Your boundaries are determined by your type of practice, and how you run your business, but also by your life experiences, needs, values and beliefs. It's important to look at all types of boundaries—those that are physical, emotional, intellectual, sexual, and energetic.

Sometimes we assume that our clients know what our boundaries are, but in fact, their boundaries are different. Good communication is very important between practitioner/therapist and client. One way to create and maintain healthy boundaries is to establish clear communication with your clients. When you articulate your information clearly, respectfully, and in a sincere tone of voice, your clients take you seriously.

When boundary issues become a problem, it often begins with gradual violations and may not present too many problems at first. But if you are the one whose boundaries are being breached, then you need to be the one to rectify the situation in a direct and non-threatening way. Clients may take advantage of you if you are not clear about your boundaries. They might be uncomfortable because your boundaries are either too restricting or too weak. This can cause confusion and you could lose clients or be overwhelmed by the results of your lack of boundaries.

The solution is to create healthy boundaries up front. Prepare a handout for clients that explains what they can expect from a session: cost, time, the flow, etc. You might state that you expect payment at the beginning of the session and explain what your "no show" policy is. You could include your work hours and times as well as when it is appropriate to call you. You could even list a telephone consultation fee for clients who tend to turn phone calls into mini-sessions. By distributing such a handout you're communicating to clients that you are very serious about your business. Along with the handout you could include an article that you have written about your service, which includes a list of benefits clients might expect to receive. When you make appointments or accept payment, do so outside the treatment area. This simple procedure creates a non-verbal boundary about what needs to be addressed outside the treatment area.

When I began setting up my full time energy business, I left a lot of room in my schedule to take clients. I would take clients on weekdays, evenings and weekends. What I found was that I was scheduling appointments according to my client's wishes instead of my own. There is a fine line here. What I have learned is that I needed to have a set schedule of times and days that I was available. In the early days, I also used to post my calendar on the wall in clear view of clients. That was a big mistake. My clients would look at it and figure that any open time slots were theirs for the taking. I soon got an appointment date book, and now I am the only one opening and closing it.

Many practitioners do not set boundaries because they are trying to grow their business and please everyone. They might see clients at times outside of their regular hours. After a while, they no longer have regular hours. They are seeing clients seven days a week, mornings, afternoons, and evenings. Their clients dictate their schedule. Their schedule will be broken up; whereby, they might have one person scheduled right in the middle of Sunday afternoon breaking up the whole day.

Some practitioners with low self-esteem have a hard time saying no and standing up for what is best for their business. They can't say no, so they are directed by the whim of their clients. What I see in this instance is that they usually charge less than what other practitioners are charging and they do a lot of sessions for free. Not that I have anything against doing Reiki for free. However, if this is your business, your scheduled time for clients is not for freebies. Free appointments are limited to a certain amount a month, at times that are convenient for you. Or you can direct the person to a local Reiki share.

Another important boundary is for clients who want to discuss their problems and difficulties with you. We have to expect that clients will want to share their problems. It's natural in an arena in which energy is moving around in the body that emotional issues will surface. While it's tempting to want to help out, keep in mind that you need to respect the limits of your own field here. If you are not a trained counselor, you need to refrain from giving advice as if you were one. It works the other way, just because clients want to share their problems with you, doesn't mean that they expect that you will share yours with them. Clients come to you to feel better, not worse, and it won't do them any good to be convinced that you are worse off than they. Above all, adhere strictly to a code of client/practitioner privacy. Make sure that you do not repeat what clients share with you.

Be sure you have thought through your policy about the time you'll allot outside of sessions. Your clients or students may feel so good after a session or a class that they may want to hang out afterward just to chat. Other clients may want to talk and talk when they call to make an appointment. The challenge is to find clever and respectful ways to handle these situations. One practitioner shared with me that she makes the following statement toward the end of a session: "We have five minutes left in this session, is there anything else we need to address here?" Or sometimes she just says, "It is time to wrap this up."

When the session is over and the client is off the table, I will schedule their next session and thank them for coming. When I feel everything is complete I begin directing them to the front door as I walk toward it. Sometimes you just have to come right out and say, "I am expecting another client soon and I need to get ready for them."

Be aware of how much telephone and text time you give to clients. Some clients seem to expect that they can have a free phone session. Help them to get to the point of their call. Learn creative and respectful ways to keep your calls short and to the point. If you encounter a client in public, don't begin a conversation about their issues as they may feel you have opened the door to free session time. It's also disrespectful of client privacy to discuss their issues in public.

If you have a client who makes you feel uncomfortable, feel free to refer them to someone else. Maybe a certain client has issues that are similar to your own, and that's why you feel uncomfortable or it may be that you just aren't meant to work with that person. I had a client who wanted me to fix her multiple emotional issues by doing soul retrieval work. She was taking many different medications to manage her depression and rages and I felt as though I did not have the expertise to handle her condition. I was comfortable doing Reiki with her, but did not want to offer any other services because I did not want to tip the delicate balance that her other therapists were trying to maintain. I told her right up front that I was only comfortable with providing Reiki.

A holistic business that supports both you and your client is grounded in and guided by respecting and maintaining healthy boundaries. Many enthusiastic therapists and practitioners, with big hearts, aspiring to make the world a better place and bring healing to others, begin a business without establishing healthy boundaries. They might not even know what their personal boundaries are until months into their practice when they notice that something is out of balance. There are several types of boundaries that need to be considered to maintain balance in our lives and in those of our clients. These include physical, emotional, intellectual, energetic, and sexual boundaries. These are examples of not having established proper boundaries:

- You enjoy providing your services to others, but you sometimes feel overextended, tired, or nearly burned out.
- You have a manageable schedule, yet at the end of the day your energy feels diminished and your joy for working is missing.
- You enjoy giving your service, but after treating some clients, you don't feel good about how your boundaries were not honored. You might even feel used or diminished in some way.

- Your clients or students take up a lot of your time outside of their scheduled appointments or class.
- You take phone calls and respond to texts at all hours.
- You agree to see clients at times that are outside of your normal work schedule.
- Your client leaves and you feel as if you have caught the ailment that they came in to have treated. You might feel their pain in your body.
- You have no free time to yourself.

The term "transference" comes from psychotherapy and is integral in determining the relationship between practitioner and client. One aspect of transference occurs when a client tries to make a professional relationship into a personal one. When this situation occurs, you may find that your client brings you gifts, asks you to lunch, or initiates personal, non-session-related conversations. It's important to remember that you are in charge of the relationship with your client. Make decisions based on your comfort level and on your respect for your own boundaries. For example, you may enjoy an occasional lunch with a client, but if it turns out that he or she just wants a great deal of free advice or wants to dump a lot of personal issues on you, you may have to learn to say no.

When you develop a friendship with a client, it changes the dynamic. This is especially true should you decide to date a client. If this is the case, make sure you refer him or her to another practitioner. When boundaries become an issue, remember that you can refer them to someone else. In some cases, this is a legal requirement depending on your licensing. It is essential to your own success to respect your clients' boundaries. However, when a client cannot respect your boundaries, remember it is perfectly alright to refer them to someone else. If you find that you have a hard time defining boundaries or saying no, consider getting some counseling on the issue. This is a sign that you have some inner work to do.

A successful business is built on knowing your boundaries and creating situations that work within those boundaries. Your clients are not expecting you to be anything other than their therapist or practitioner. They will not know your boundaries unless you provide them – clearly and respectfully. What they are looking for is your service and any information that you may access while working with them that will help them feel better, heal, or have greater insight. Maintaining healthy boundaries is a vital part of taking care of yourself. When you are healthy, happy, and feeling in balance, you will draw to you clients that will want your services. If you are run down and out of synch with life, your client base will diminish.

It is also important to understand that your client has boundaries. You want to make sure that you are not violating their boundaries. If you are not sure about how they will react to something, ask. Listen when they are speaking to you. A lot of information about their boundaries is being offered. Ask if you are unclear. When I have a first time Reiki client, I explain how I work and the options of hands on or off the body. I will ask if it is ok with them if I do the sessions with hands on the body. When you honor their boundaries, they feel safe and will return. If you do not, they will most likely not return.

SELF CARE

Self-care is a vital part of running a successful business. Self-care means taking care of your physical body and your emotional needs and it means taking a vacation once in a while. As you share the benefits of your modality to others, make sure that you too are receiving bodywork of some kind on a regular basis.

When you are self-employed no one is going to tell you that you need a day off or a vacation, so it's important to be in touch with your overall health and well-being. You need to make sure that you are taking days off to have fun, not just days off to do your books. If you are depleted, your clients will not benefit from what you are offering. And if you push yourself too hard, you could end up in a healing crisis and be unable to work.

Self-care also means being true to your boundaries. As I grew with my business, I learned to make some self-care adjustments with regard to my business. I stopped scheduling appointments on weekends. I also learned that I needed to give myself one day off a week, sometimes more, especially when I would be teaching on weekends. I occasionally plan trips on weekends, when I am not teaching workshops, to reenergize. I also choose to be around people that I really enjoy when I am not working. I make it a priority to go to the park or the woods or to be near the water as often as possible.

Sometimes allowing space and time to be alone or to get a massage or acupuncture is a great way to do something good for you. Quiet time allows you to recharge, clear your mind, find balance, and connect with inner thoughts and ideas that will guide your business decisions. It's so important to take care of yourself and to avoid pushing yourself past your limits. A sick healer does not make the world a better place. Think about how your clients will feel if you appear exhausted or disheveled or if you spend the session coughing and sneezing.

What I see with a lot of entrepreneurs, is that they forget how to have fun. They are so busy being busy. I find that entrepreneurs in the holistic field are wired for giving and caring. And even though this is good, it can be a downfall. I find that many practitioners, on what is to be their day off, are taking care of family members, running errands for others, or are on the phone all day with clients. Not a true day off.

In your mind, work with the word "fun." What does that mean to you? How can you find more fun in your life? Fun is an attitude. Your work can be heavy or it can be fun. Find ways to generate more fun in all areas of your life. I bought a $15 drum that looks like a lollipop. It is almost a foot around and is lightweight. Right now it sits on my dining room table. I find myself beating it several times throughout the day. It is fun, raises my energy, and makes me smile. I also get great ideas after beating it.

When you are having fun, you smile. Your clients can see if you are rested and taking care of yourself. If I had a practitioner that looked exhausted or disinterested, I would stop going.

Exercise 18: Taking Care of Yourself - List some activities that you currently do that help you to find balance and reenergize.

List some other activities you might want to consider in order to expand your ability to find balance and to stay healthy.

List activities that bring you JOY. Engage in them often!

List activities that rob you of energy. Consider releasing these activities from your life.

You are under no obligation to allow others to take your energy or to wear you down. You are allowed to have healthy boundaries.

Starters, Growers, Expanders – Take an internal inventory. What do you need to do to regenerate, balance, relax, and have fun? Build this into your schedule. Make it happen and you will be more successful, live longer and be happier.

CAREER OR CALLING?

There are generally two motivations for why practitioners/therapists choose to work in the field of holistic health. In the first instance, you might have chosen a particular modality from a variety of career options. You might have chosen this profession early in life, when you were just out of high school or college. Or you may have found this specialty later in life as a part of your own healing practice or as a way to transition out of a toxic work environment into one you believed to be more supportive of yourself or others. You see your profession as a job or career that will support you financially.

Or you might have a different motivation: you may practice your modality because you were called to do so. I have heard many practitioners say—and this was true in my case—"I did not choose it. It chose me." Their business is their *calling*. They don't believe that their modality is work, per se, but instead they perform this work because they cannot *not* perform it. Their work is more than a physical, emotional, or mental desire to help others; it is a spiritual path that impacts both the client and the practitioner.

Now there are benefits and drawbacks to each of these situations. The career-oriented practitioner brings a lot of excitement and enthusiasm to share with his clients. He/she is open to learning and growing in many ways to become a better therapist to help others. A key to his success is that he/she is willing to work very hard to create a successful business. His/her motivation is usually to help others, to make money and possibly to make a name for himself/herself. No one can be faulted for viewing their business in this fashion. All practitioners need to support themselves and should do so abundantly. Working to make a name for yourself can be a noble thing. Although many career-oriented practitioners are very intuitive and acknowledge a belief and faith in God or a higher power as support for their success, they tend to rely on their intellect and hard work to manifest results.

Career-oriented practitioners measure their success by the tangible things that manifest from their actions, such as money, status, assets, or material goods. The key for those focusing on career is to avoid getting caught up in fear or anxiety, when on any given day a client cancels or plans go awry. In these instances, it won't help to place blame or to focus on ways in which abundance is being blocked for you. Focus instead on the many ways you can respond to a situation. You can become anxious, terminate relationships, impede progress or you can generate grace and gratitude and build rapport and abundance.

If you focus on negative events, you can create negative cash flow situations. Instead of focusing on the negative and manifesting fear, focus on the positive. If you put a lot of energy into thinking about your fears, you can end up attracting these fear-based situations to yourself.

Say, for example, you become anxious or depressed because a client canceled or decided not to use your services anymore. The fear created by your anxiety may attract more clients to cancel. Or say a receptionist in the spa or center where you work didn't inform you about an early morning appointment, and you show up 10 minutes late and find the client waiting. Instead of greeting the client, you get angry with the receptionist rather than connecting with the paying client and with the flow of that moment. You end up putting out negative energy around the situation, which can bring negative energy into your business and into the spa or center where you work. If you start imagining future negative scenarios ("What if this continues to happen?" or "I could have lost the client") the accumulated bad energy can sink a business. You'll be thinking, "I have the right training and I did all the right things, but what went wrong?" Instead of seeing the glass half empty, see it half full and rising toward the brim. For those who are career-focused practitioners, it's very important to cultivate an inner, positive attitude of creating abundance and to see challenges and errors along the path as a sea of opportunities for learning, expansion, and growth. It will be very helpful for you to create a balance between hard work and trusting your inner connection with spirit to manifest your desired outcome.

Those involved in the holistic health field because it is a calling, are motivated by their desire to help others and to serve humanity. Money is not the bottom line and most do not fear not having money. They know that their God or Higher Self connection and faith will create the circumstances in which abundance flows. Clients benefit from these practitioners' intuitive connection with the spirit of all life. For those who are answering a calling, the key to success is that they can see a bigger picture. They create that picture by putting out a clear intention to Spirit and then watching it manifest in remarkable ways. Their faith is a grounding factor in their success. If you're among this latter group, then your reaction to the negative situation described above might be very different. You know that there is a reason for everything even if you do not know why it happens. Instead of getting caught up in trying to find an explanation for an event like the miscommunication between receptionist and therapist described above, you make the best of what happens, knowing that what is unfolding is perfect. If you do get caught in such an experience, you quickly release the negative energy and ask, what am I to learn from this situation? You work hard, but a lot of your work begins in the inner working of co-creating with Spirit and responding to life on all levels from the inner cues that you receive.

Practitioners with a calling are sometimes accused of not being business minded or not accepting payment for what they are worth. They may also be perceived as needy or as overly dependent on clients to validate their need to be of service. If they don't take care of the details of running a business or refuse to accept equal exchange for what their service is worth, practitioners can also sink themselves financially. When a calling is what supports these practitioners' way of life, they need to attend to the practical day-to-day details of running a business with the same attention and focus that supports and motivates them to serve. They must also heal any neediness issues, or clients will feel the unhealthy energy and quickly end the relationship.

Both of these motivations—career and calling—are equally valid. Neither motivation is right or wrong. It is what has gotten all of us here on this path today. Both perspectives can create abundant flourishing businesses. The lesson here is that we need to understand how our motivations support or sabotage our business.

It is wonderful to have such a plethora of holistic health practitioners and to have the opportunity to learn from those around us. Ask yourself why you choose the services of those practitioners you frequent for your own wellness. Think about those whom you view as successful practitioners and ask yourself what you can learn from observing them. What are your strengths and weaknesses? Look at your own attitudes and perceptions, at how you see your business and your clients. Are there fears within that are hampering your success? What now-dormant quality can be awakened to support your success? Such qualities are in every one of us. No matter what our motivating factors are, let us support the success of all practitioners and therapists in this noble field of healing humanity!

One last point about the situation in which the receptionist forgot to give the message to the practitioner. There are many ways that the situation could have been handled. The truth is that whether we regard our business as career or calling, we are all 100% responsible for delivering our thoughts and ideas clearly and for assuring that the listener receives them correctly. If the receptionist failed to give us a message or we find ourselves caught up in a miscommunication, then we must ask ourselves why it is happening. Look at the facts and then take full responsibility for bringing a positive solution to the table. Address the situation as quickly as possible in order to prevent a recurrence of the event. This is a great way to provide the quickest solution with the least amount of stress for all concerned and it is a beneficial way to continue the successful flow of your holistic business.

Good communication skills are imperative in our line of work. You not only need to know what to say and how to say it, but you also need to speak up when it counts. Many of us have become an expert in refraining from communicating with others, but such behavior usually ends up conveying mixed signals or blocking important exchanges. For those who work in close proximity with others, good communication skills can really improve everyone's comfort level; by the same token, poor communication can result in confusion and frustration. Communicating clearly with honesty and respect can also help to collectively harness the energy in a workplace and to bolster everyone's success.

INNER WORK FOR SUCCESS IN BUSINESS

We all know that in running a business, the outer work that we do is detrimental to our success. A lot of the time we forget that the work that we do inside is just as important for our success, if not more so.

Inner Factors for Creating a Success Business

Becoming successful in any field or endeavor does not happen by luck. Hard work and determination might be where some people would begin. However, there are several key inner factors that set apart those who become successful in creating a business. Statistics show that four out of five small businesses fail within the first two years of operation. When you look at someone with a successful business, his or her secrets are not always on the surface. Success factors cannot always be seen because the winning combination starts within.

The first key to having a successful business is to take time each morning imagining how you are going to fulfill the vision that you have for your business.

The success of your business is also determined by your inner motivator. What language does your inner motivator speak? Does your inner motivator talk in positive and realistic terms about life, about business and about your success? Does your inner motivator speak positively about others in the field? The inner voice that motivates you to success is your main supporter and cheerleader. Consciously take time and listen to the messages your inner motivator is sending. Successful people are self-motivated and see the glass is filled to top with plenty for everyone in the field. If you are speaking negatively, turn it around, or pick another direction.

Get grounded. If you are not grounded and are floating around in a spacy place in your head or outside of it, nothing will get done and you will not impress anyone. Some practitioners believe that their clients want someone who is over the top spiritual. That is not true. Your clients want someone who is present, listens to them, and can respond accordingly. If you are not grounded, your business will fail and your clients will go elsewhere. Whether you have a spiritual or energy based modality or not, running a business is a grounded affair. If you are depending on this to make a living, get yourself grounded. If you need help getting grounded, get it.

Next on the inner realms, exam your views about money and success. What I have found is that some people on a subconscious level have taken an oath of poverty. Other people believe, if they have money, others are doing without. Then there is the self-defeating attitude about money and success, which is that their money goals are out of reach or that they will never be successful. Money is a form of energy, which is an exchange for a service. I work using my energy, and I receive money as a form of exchange. If you have something worthwhile to offer, then money is the proper form of exchange. Stop blocking the flow of energy (money) into your life. Look within at your attitude toward money and success.

Another inner factor key to success is to activate your awareness. Day-to-day we fill each moment with a lot of busyness that does not relate to our vision or goals. Old habits of talking on the phone, texting, or running other people's errand because that is what we are used to, will not create success. By eliciting your inner awareness to watch your day-to-day activities, to make sure those activities are directed toward completing your vision, goals and strategies, will ensure that you stay on track for success. Do not criticize yourself. This is a learning process to make you more aware of how you are spending your time and energy. You are learning to make better choices. Allow your inner awareness to guide you to release the activities and people that do not serve your vision. You will experience more energy for reaching your potential success.

Aligning With Greatness

Everything has energy. Even our words and thoughts have energy. They too create a response in the outer world. The act of comparing ourselves or *measuring up* to others creates a profoundly negative energy that affects our ability to succeed. Even though the world that you live in with commercials, billboards, and the news emphasizes what everyone else is doing and what they have, aligning with your inner greatness requires that you release this need to compare.

Somewhere we learned to judge our success by comparing ourselves to others. We were not born with the comparison gene, we were taught this by our family and society. We were taught to strive for what other's defined as bringing happiness or notoriety. We seem to get stuck on how we *measure up* against our competition, family members, or friends: why someone prefers their talents over yours, how much money someone else is making versus what you earned or how big their home is or the car brand they drive versus the one you own.

This can make you feel as if you are never going to reach your goals leaving you disappointed as you strive to be like someone else instead of being yourself. Comparison creates the energy of frustration, discontentment and let down, polluting your path with an energy that drains you from the life force necessary to create success. You compare yourself to others even though your needs and desires are different. Spending useless time comparing apples to oranges, takes you further away from reaching your real goals.

This treadmill of *measuring up* to others' definition of success is never ending. It creates an energy within you of *lack* and *judgment*. Untangle yourself from this sticky web that keeps you trapped in someone else's definitions by stepping out of the energy of comparing. Right now release that negative mindset that continues to create limitations.

Your success is all about you, not someone else that you might idolize. Align with your Inner Greatness that is naturally a part of your make up. Minus comparison, focus on your inner strengths that fire your success engine. Begin by asking yourself, "What does success mean to me?" "What is my ultimate image of how success looks in my work life, home life, and relationship life?" "What are my strengths?" "What is unique about me?" "What areas do I need to improve and what resources are needed to help me to improve in these areas?" "How can I effectively use my inner and outer resources to reach my goals?"

Count your past successes. Acknowledge them and smile. Align with the Greatness that is uniquely you. Let the energy of these successes stoke the internal fires to energize you to move forward. Step into this flow that comes from within and let it guide and direct your next steps. Align your mind to consciously choose the ideas and thoughts that support only success.

Make sure that you are being realistic with your goals based on where you are, the energy that you are investing toward your goals, and the amount of energy needed to accomplish your goals. Leave timelines open. Pressuring yourself with strict timeframes compresses energy and can drain you of the valuable energy that you need to accomplish your goals. Be open to the greatness within to provide you with creative ideas and inspiration.

YOU are an incredible brilliant and creative person. Release the need to compare, *measure up* to, or judge yourself. This will free up your energy and allow you to express your gifts, wisdom, and creativity that are unique to you. Success will define itself in its own distinctive way, which may not look like anything that anyone else is doing. You might just be pleasantly surprised with how it all unfolds without as much effort and drama as you previously believed it might be.

The world around you is constantly changing. Therefore, you must continuously evaluate your goals, energy level, desires, needs, likes and dislikes and change accordingly. The energy of Greatness is within you. It is just waiting for an opening, so that it can be released to support all of your dreams. You can open that door now and align with this Greatness or continue to wait another week or year, as you look to others to define you. Answer the call for success and happiness by aligning with the energy of Greatness within, letting it flow and energize into all areas of your life.

Navigating the Road to Success

Have you ever felt stuck? That a big boulder was blocking your way? You push and work even harder, but success feels elusive? What do you do? Give up, work harder, or create another plan?

Success is more than reaching the final goal. It is a process. Success comes from knowing when to push harder, when to rest, reflect, plan and when to connect with others. Like driving through a city, you need to stop at the red lights and wait until it is time to proceed. Some red lights are longer than others. But it is imperative that you stop or you could get injured. You will reach your final destination if you pay attention to the signs along the way.

Life occurs in phases. There is the hard working phase, the rest and reflection, the networking and connecting with others, and the learning and planning phase. Most of the time these stages overlap to some degree. Being able to identify which phase(s) you are in so that you can apply your energy appropriately is very important. This will help you to direct your energy. The hard working phase has to have some endings or you will burn out before you find your success. When this phase is working for you, everything seems to fall into place. You naturally know what is next because it presents itself to you. There is a quickening of events.

This is usually followed by the rest and reflection phase. The rest and reflection stage is essential! This is where you listen deeply to your inner knowing, making space for it to present new ideas and information about your path. You reflect on what is and is not working. You don't try to "fix" things. You open to new ways of being or handling issues. It is important to rest your mind so that you can get in touch with your higher thoughts and wisdom. This is what fuels your next steps. If you refuse to pause, you risk the chance of hitting a roadblock and experiencing anxiety and despair. Your inner voice tells you to stop, go, talk to this person, attend this meeting, etc. If you don't listen to it, you are traveling without your GPS turned on. Listen to you inner wisdom.

The networking and connecting with like-minded people phase also supports your success. We do not exist in a vacuum. We learn and are blessed by the company of others. Connect with positive people who share and support your vision. Do not spend time with negative people who steal your energy and bring you down. Many times someone holds the answer to some question. Change can occur more quickly when group minds are at work. Moving that mountain seems less hard when you have a team behind you. Spend time with like-minded people and be energized by the time you spend with them.

The learning and planning phase usually occurs before the hard working phase and after the rest and reflection stage. It is important to take the time to acknowledge what you learned from your experiences and revise your plans according to how the path now presents itself. This phase allows you to respond to the changes going on in your environment. Nothing is static. The world around you is in constant change and this phase allows you to plan accordingly.

When you identify and participate in all the phases, you will no longer feel frustrated and stuck. You feel empowered to take the steps that are appropriate for that phase. This will propel you on your road to success.

Fueling Your Success

Your success depends on how much physical, emotional, and mental energy that you have to support your passion and goals. If the tank is empty, the car won't start. In order to stay the course and fuel your passion, you need energy to sustain all levels of your being.

The human body is not only biological (bones, skin, etc.) and chemical (hormones, blood and other bodily fluids); it is also energetic. Each person has an energy field called an aura that surrounds the body and inwardly fuels the body, mind and emotions to create health and vitality. Without a healthy energy field the body begins to breakdown physically and emotionally into dis-eased states.

Each person has seven main energy centers called chakras located in the central core of the body: one at the base of the spine, the second at the naval, third at the solar plexus, fourth at the heart, fifth at the throat, sixth at the center of the forehead, and the seventh at the crown of the head. These centers regulate and move energy into all parts of the body, providing fuel for all aspects of our being. If one or more of the chakras become blocked or depleted because of lifestyle choices you make, you can begin to tire, feel anxiety, and over time disease develops.

Stress, poor diet, excess caffeine and sugar, lack of exercise, smoking, drugs, too much alcohol, worry, fear, depression, anger, and environmental and energetic pollutants are just a few factors that will delete the body's energy and create energy blocks. You may not experience low energy or imbalance at first when you engage in these activities, but over time one of the above factors, singly or in combination, will cause your energy to falter. You feel as if your get up and go got up and left. Your flame, fueling your drive for success has gone out and it is a struggle to get back into the groove of in success. Signs of illness and imbalance indicate that your energy centers are blocked or diminished.

There are many things that you can do to increase and enhance your energetic system. Reduce stress, walk, exercise, adjust your diet, meditate, receive a Reiki session or massage, smile, yoga, deep breathing, counseling or life coaching, and detox the body. Look at what is out of balance in your life and work to bring it back into balance. Take a three to seven day retreat and detoxify your mind of limiting beliefs, fear, and worry. Walk in nature and receive the energy that connecting with the earth, air, water, and sun can provide you naturally. When you can detoxify your life from the habits that create energy blocks, you are rejuvenated and your energy is restored.

Create a vision of yourself that supports vibrant energy. What would that look like? How would that feel in your body, mind, and emotions? How would you experience yourself with a full tank of energy that does not come from coffee or another stimulant? Take a few moments and get in touch with your vision. Write it down and claim it for yourself. Take the steps necessary to realign with this energy to support your passion and success. Affirm, envision and feel that "I am a vibrant being filled with energy, love, and passion to fulfill my goals and ensure my success. I make healthy choices every day to support my path to success." Take some time to breathe these affirmations into each chakra and smile on your road to success.

If you do any type of energy work, make sure you are doing this on yourself. Make a daily practice of giving yourself energy at the beginning and the end of each day. Have a daily practice of disconnecting from your clients and work at the end of each day.

Becoming a Magnet for Success

When you clear the blocked up energy and open up the chakras to support your goals, you can go one step further to make life a lot easier. You fill your auric field with gratitude, love, and peace. When you genuinely fill your energy field with these qualities and respond to life with these positive attributes, you initiate a chain reaction.

Energy follows thoughts and actions. Aligning your energy with gratitude, love, and peace empowers and expands your energy field. Your vibration rises and you attract all that is necessary to reach your goals. The stumbling blocks seem to disappear. What once seemed difficult becomes easy. Your fortified field acts like a magnet because it is so clear and the energy is so enhanced by these higher vibrational qualities.

Look at your life and focus on what you are grateful for. Be grateful for the success that you know is yours. Be grateful for all your clients, coworkers, and management. Be grateful for the wonderful opportunity that you are given. Find gratitude in your heart for everything and share it with others. Tell your family, clients, coworkers, and friends how thankful you are for their presence in your life. Raise the energy and vibration of gratitude in your energy field by living in deep appreciation for the experience you are having.

Real love has no conditions. Love is without judgment. Activate the power of love to raise your energy by focusing this power into everything that you do. Replace the feelings of frustration, impatience, indifference, and criticism to being and extending love. Love shifts the energy to magnetizing to you your highest good.

Peace brings balance to all aspects of your being. It creates a foundation that allows you to make decisions from a place of power and not fear. It liberates you from acting on what others think you should do and provides a strong inner knowing to stay your course. Peace is freedom. It gives you flexibility to change and grow on your journey to success.

After you activate these qualities as part of your life on a daily basis, you lift the heavy feelings that have imprisoned you into limiting your success. With gratitude, love, and peace filling your being, the energy in response to your intentions speeds up. Your creativity and intuition open to support your goals. Your wisdom provides a wealth of knowledge because it is given a field in which it can have a voice.

Your energy becomes a gift that you give to others and the world around you. The universe responds with the right people showing up, contracts being filled, opportunities appearing, loving relationships, abundance streaming in, etc. You feel satisfaction and contentment along the way.

Take an inventory of what your energy field is filled with and begin enhancing it with the power and energy of gratitude, love, and peace. It will make the journey to success easier, joy filled, and unpredictably satisfying. Experience yourself as a magnet with these high vibrational qualities attracting your highest good and success.

CULTIVATE SUCCESS, BE SUCCESS

No two minds ever come together without thereby creating a third, invisible intangible force, which may be likened to a third mind." — Napoleon Hill

Mastermind Groups

The secret to creating success for some people is that they surround themselves with positive, intelligent and intuitive people who provide honest feedback and ideas. Mastermind groups came about in the early 1900s for the purpose of tapping into a larger body of knowledge and the experience of business-savvy folks from a variety of backgrounds. Groups met on a weekly basis and provided support and information/resources to the person who had convened the group. Groups of up to 50 people provided advice and insight. The concept is believed to be drawn from the model of a king who sought advice from the Knights of the Round Table.

The first time I read about Mastermind groups was in Napoleon Hill's *Think and Grow Rich*. Hill was fortunate enough to shadow the successful entrepreneur Andrew Carnegie for 20 years to study the factors that made Carnegie successful. Hill contends that part of Carnegie's success stemmed from the support that Carnegie received from his Mastermind group. On a regular basis, Carnegie would assemble a group of 50 people with expertise in various fields. He would share with them his goals and plans and would elicit their ideas and feedback. He even paid some members to be a part of the group. He would listen to what the group members had to say and then make decisions accordingly, based on the information that he gathered at the meetings, and based on his knowledge, experience and intuition on these matters.

Mastermind groups still operate today and they aren't just for the wealthy; they can really benefit holistic health practitioners. You don't need a large group and you can reconfigure your own group so that it supports the success of all members instead of just one person. The group can take time to focus on each individual, brainstorming ideas to help him or her attain their vision and goals. The Mastermind members can also manifest the collective energy of the group to focus it on supporting each member.

Mastermind groups working in this new paradigm should be small (fewer than 10 members) and should agree to a regular meeting time (once a week, twice a month, or once a month) and duration (allowing about 20 to 30 minutes per person). It might vary depending on the needs of the group. Group members should not all be acupuncturists or all Reiki practitioners, but should be a mix of different therapists with varying backgrounds.

The group should serve all members' needs and support the success of each member's business vision and goals. When the group gets together, each person, one at a time, should share her vision and her goals. If she is stuck in some area or needs advice, she can ask the group. The group listens and holds all comments and advice until the person is finished speaking. Then each member is given the opportunity to provide constructive feedback. After all dialog is completed, the group members silently visualize the complete success of the person who just spoke or goes into the silence to seek any intuitive messages. After all sharing is completed, the energy moves to the next person to share her business plans, goals, concerns or questions.

It is important to make sure the group stays on task, so it can be helpful to allot a specific time that will be spent addressing each individual. Because it's tempting to start talking about unrelated activities, you might want to meet 20 minutes ahead of time to get the chit chat out of the way or to share a meal afterward in order to socialize. At the end of the meeting, sit in the silence and visualize the group members being successful in their services. Visualize all practitioners being successful.

Leave the door open for the group to experience creative activities that will support growth and inspiration. You may decide to see a movie together that supports what the group is about or you may want to experience a meditation together. The group should be open and flexible to participating in activities that supports members' growth and learning. When members want the group to try something new, make sure everyone is in agreement. You want to build synergy, not lose energy. Members should be dedicated to attending for the good of their own business and for the good of all.

Many business owners are very busy, so adding another event to go out to would be too much. There are mastermind groups online that meets on Facetime, Skype or Zoom to mastermind their way to success. There are some that you pay to be a part of that are led by leaders in the industry.

I'd like to share with you Mary Robinson Reynolds' seven steps to Masterminding. Please see her website for more information. www.maryrobinsonreynolds.com

7 Steps to the MasterMind Connection™

I SURRENDER ordinary thinking. I recognize and accept that I desire to add to my own inherent power the sum and substance of the intelligence, experience, knowledge and spirituality of my MasterMind partners to provide amazing ideas and affirmative language to assist me in generating new results now.

I FOCUS the power of my intention to be open to all possibilities. I dissolve in my mind, and in the minds of all others, any idea that my own good can be withheld from me. No person, thing or event can keep that from me, which the power of the creative mechanism of our collective minds – the MasterMind –can conceive of, and bring me in perfect timing.

I DECIDE differently. Within and without, I call all things past, all things present, all things future, a success. I release positively everyone. I am free and they are free too. All things are cleared up between us now and forever.

I KNOW that, when two or more minds come together in the spirit of harmony, peace and goodwill, the accomplishment of my goals, dreams and desires will be intentionally created through this alliance, to bring about easy effectiveness, energy and good to all.

I ASK my partners' support in seeing and believing for me what I really want. I now make known my specific goals and requests, knowing that the accumulative MasterMind consciousness of this group will lift my thinking, shift my receptivity to what I've asked for and open my mind to creative solution-generating ideas and language.

I ACCEPT and receive all that I am aligned with. I give great appreciation to the third, invisible intangible force as it responds, in the ways that are best, to my desires. I assume the same feelings I will have as my goals and requests are being actualized.

I DEDICATE myself to be of maximum service to those around me, to be a living example of what humanity can be and to practice "harmlessness" in generating peace, love, harmony and goodwill in my world. I am grateful and relaxed ... and so it is.

I GO forth with a spirit of enthusiasm, excitement and expectancy.

I AM at peace with this or something greater.

Attitude and Intention

Attitude and intention is everything! Positive attitudes attract clients. Positive attitudes help you to expand your intentions. Think about whom the people are that you like to hang out with, do they make you feel good? What attitude do they exude? Your attitude goes beyond the timeframe of seeing clients. If you are a positive and upbeat person in most aspects of your daily life, your life will be blessed with positive outcomes surrounding your visions and intentions. It seems to me that the more love, compassion, and joy that we embody, our capacity to address the healing needs of others by the expansion of our gifts is increased.

When business is at a slow point, do not send negative thoughts to your business. Do not compare yourself to other successes and do not look at your fellow practitioners as competition. Such comparison will diminish the energy that you have and cause you to lose good friends. There are millions of people in the United States and hundreds of thousands or more within a 50-mile radius of where you live. There aren't enough hours in the day for you to treat each person, so in order to meet the need and stay healthy, you can only see a limited number of people in a week. All told, I teach about 150 new students a year as well as teach to a large number of students that return to take additional courses. There is a need for a lot of practitioners and teachers. All of us can be successful.

The clients and students you treat or teach will resonate with you. Others will resonate with someone else. As you change energetically and heal your own issues, you will find that the clients and students you attract will change also. Here is a good combination for success: market your business, trust the flow, work in integrity, honor others, and show gratitude.

Some days will present challenges and you might find yourself thinking about leaving your line of work. Just know that in every challenge lies an opportunity. You might need to adjust your work schedule to make more time for yourself. You might need to release some problematic clients who you feel you have helped all you can. You may consider shifting your marketing plan to focus on a new set of clients. But before you make any major changes, take some time to cool down and relax. Don't make any major decisions when you are upset; instead, spend some time alone and reflect. You might need to seek the advice of those whom you trust.

Make sure, that in all areas of your life, you surround yourself with healthy, supportive people. Make sure you have a couple of close friends or advisers with whom you can share your business ideas and goals. Listen to their feedback. Don't share your plans with everyone, especially those who might tend to see the glass half empty. Seek support or share your vision with those who will support you.

Don't automatically assume that an unexpected lull is bad news. It may be related to taking care of family members' needs or to some unexpected concern or maybe the universe is granting you a much-needed break. During these times, look for places to do your one-hour presentation. Improve your marketing and teaching materials. Develop new contacts. Rest and go for a walk. Meditate. Have fun. Love yourself and your business.

Build and preserve your energy at all times. Be aware of energy shifts and changes along your path. As you shift, you will be guided to meet new people, take new classes, open new doors, and shift your business.

The more love that you experience and give, the more you will attract those seeking to heal on all levels. Clients really are seeking those practitioners who radiate positive energy.

Starters – Check in on your attitude. Is it supporting what you want in life?

Growers – Join a Mastermind group, either one that is online or one that meets in person.

Expanders – Start a Mastermind group. Be a mentor to others, whether you charge for these services or not.

VISION DECLARATION REVISITED

Reread the latest version of your Vision Declaration. If it is not exactly what you are envisioning based on all that you have discovered about yourself from reading and doing the exercises in this book, then sit in the silence and write down your revised vision. Read your vision declaration on a regular basis and as it changes, take time to sit with it and rewrite your vision and revise the goals that support it.

Like a book, your business has many chapters and can be modified, changed, and enhanced. It is up to you to choose the course of action that you need to undertake in each chapter of your business. Learn to listen and trust your intuition. Be creative and original. Choose joy and happiness as the fuel that moves you forward. At the end of each day, if we don't have peace and happiness as a result of our practices, we need to ask ourselves, "Was it worth it?" I hope that your business brings you peace, joy, and success and that you can say that all of it has been worth it.

Remember we create our destiny. Success starts within and flows outward. Continue to do your inner work to create success on the outer plane.

This is not the end. It is just another beginning point for creating your successful business and for tapping into your unlimited potential.

Namaste

Appendix I: Vision Declarations, Goals and Affirmations

Example 1

Vision Declaration

I am a wildly successful businesswoman. I see 18 clients weekly in my home-based massage therapy business. I am building positive alliances with chiropractors in my area that generate a steady flow of clients. I give talks on a regular basis at health clubs in my area.

Goals

Make business cards.

Schedule appointment with chiropractors and discuss my services.

Schedule meetings with health club managers and set up speaking opportunities.

Reserve a space at the local health fair.

Make a quarter-page ad for the local health-related newspaper.

Affirmations

I am a successful massage therapist. I am speaking at health clubs about my passion. I am providing services that make my clients feel wonderful and this generates referrals to my business.

Example 2

Vision Declaration

I successfully provide Reflexology services that assist clients in healing and returning to the wholeness of body, mind and spirit. I also provide quality learning experiences to fully enrolled classes, dealing with hand and foot reflexology. I guide students to reach their full potential through mentoring programs. I publish articles, newsletters and books that serve these purposes.

Goals

Update flyers for upcoming workshops.

Schedule three talks at local hospitals to educate medical staff about the benefits of reflexology.

Schedule mentoring dates for advanced students.

Advertise upcoming classes in local newspaper.

Apply for being a CE provider for massage therapists and occupational therapists.

Affirmations

I am a successful and sought after reflexologist. I have lots of great clients and my classes are filled with students who are eager to learn. I easily complete all my goals, expanding my success in helping others to heal.

Example 3

Vision Declaration

I fill all my yoga classes. I provide deep relaxation and peace to all participants. I offer yoga programs to children as well as to adults. I offer parent/child yoga classes.

Goals

Develop yoga programs geared to children and to parent-child interaction.

Contact the nearby community college about developing a summer children's yoga camp.

Contact the local elementary schools to discuss after-school yoga programs.

Make and distribute flyers and brochures to advertise my services.

Write an article for my blog and have it published in at least two local newsletters focused on children.

Write an article for a national magazine focusing on parents/children.

Affirmations

I am an accomplished yoga teacher with fully enrolled classes. My calendar is filled with opportunities to teach both adults and children in classes together and separately.

Example 4

Vision Declaration

I have a successful and abundant holistic health center that meets my community's needs for a variety of holistic health options. I have at least six practitioners who offer a combination of massage, acupuncture, Reiki, Healing Touch, nutritional counseling and reflexology. My center offers workshops that are filled to capacity.

Goals

Research the county's regulations regarding opening up a holistic healing center.

Consult with an SBA counselor.

Meet with my accountant.

Sign a lease for the space.

Work with architect for the design of the build of the space.

Affirmations

I am the owner of Annapolis Holistic Health Center, a successful center that provides a mixture of desired holistic services. The community abundantly supports the Center and all the practitioners and the owner are prosperous. The energy extended in this Center provides light and healing to all. I am outrageously successful and a great mentor for other holistic health providers.

Appendix II: Chamber of Commerce Benefits

Below is an example of the many benefits that you can receive from joining your local Chamber of Commerce. Search for your local Chamber of Commerce online. The information below was taken from the Northern Anne Arundel County Chamber of Commerce (NAACCC) website. www.naaccc.com.

Membership Benefit

Membership with NAACCC doesn't Cost, It PAYS.

NAACCC Membership Directory: Our Directory is a valuable resource that connects you with your fellow Chamber members. It is also your reference for potential clients and business services.

The Chamber Connection: Our monthly newsletter, published in the Maryland Gazette, reaches over 38,000 residents and businesses. Discounted advertising is available to Chamber members.

Website: Chamber members receive a free link on our website. Use this valuable tool to promote your business.

Credibility: As a Chamber member, you are part of an association of business leaders working toward improving the county's economy and quality of life.

Networking: Chamber members increase their business contacts and develop valuable relationships through participation at our networking events. Multi-Chamber Networking Breakfasts help you reach businesses outside our local area. General Membership Luncheons feature interesting speakers and networking opportunities. After-Hours Business Mixers give you an opportunity to meet other Chamber members and network in a relaxed atmosphere.

Credit Card Payment: Chamber members can easily register and pay for events or services by using their credit cards.

Business Referrals: People do business with people they know. Get known as a business leader within the Chamber and the referrals will start coming in.

Relocation Information: New residents coming into the county can receive information about Chamber businesses, as well as county services.

Certificate of Origin: This service is available to Chamber members for a small fee.

Advocacy: Our Legislative Committee has a direct voice to federal, state, and local officials on issues that affect you and your business.

Referral Groups: As a member of one of our three free Referral Groups, you will be sharing ideas, tools of the trade and techniques of your business.

Chamber Committees: Expand your networking opportunities by taking an active role in the Chamber's 12 special events and standing committees.

Ribbon Cutting Ceremonies: Bring Chamber members and the community to your new business. The ceremony includes the presentation of Citations from local politicians.

Meet Dawn Fleming

Dawn Fleming has been working in the field of holistic health care since 1989. Dawn is an Usui and Karuna Reiki® Master, medical intuitive, life coach, and sound therapist. She is the Director of Energy Transformations, where she offers services and classes that empower and inspire health and well-being. Dawn has studied Chakra Balancing, Therapeutic Touch, Cranial-Sacral Therapy, Usui, Reiki, Karuna Reiki®, Medical Intuition, and Hypnotherapy. She teaches and mentors many therapists to create successful businesses.

For the left-brain world, Dawn has a Bachelor's degree in Business Management, has completed some work at the Masters level, and worked for 20 years in the federal government as a Senior Intelligence Analyst as well as a Senior Policy Officer. In 2001, she followed her higher calling and resigned from her full-time job to expand her healing and teaching work, which was previously a part-time pursuit. Since 2001, her private business has grown to full-time and the number of workshops and speaking opportunities has expanded as well. She is currently developing online classes. The experience of developing her own successful business, combined with her love of writing and teaching, led Dawn to develop this book as a great resource and guide for holistic health practitioners and therapists.

Her goal is to help therapists and practitioners in the field of holistic health/integrative medicine to build amazing businesses. Through her services, Dawn shares her knowledge through workshops and writing. To learn more about her workshops visit:

http://www.energytransformations.org.

Resources created by Dawn Fleming to Assist Your Success

Reiki I and II manuals (spiral bound) that Reiki Masters can use to make copies of for their students.

Teaching Workshops Effectively book

Mastering Reiki book

Mastering Reiki DVD

Chakra Empowerment: 24 Days of Transformation

Meditations for Success (CD) with five meditations

Check out her online classes which offer CEs for massage therapists

Chakra Awakening: Create Health and Well Being Naturally

Reiki Summit Wisdom Package – video interviews of Reiki experts and bonus materials.

How to Become a Continuing Education Provider

Above and Beyond: Distance Reiki Techniques

The online classes can be joined at

http://energy-transformations.teachable.com/

Visit my website for these amazing books to further your success.

http://www.energytransformations.org

www.ingramcontent.com/pod-product-compliance
Lightning Source LLC
Chambersburg PA
CBHW022057210326
41519CB00054B/564